Journals and Journalism

Keep this book under
a weight until thoroughly
dry, otherwise the binding
will warp.

Journals
and Journalism:

With a Guide for Literary Beginners.

BY
JOHN OLDCASTLE.

1880.

SECOND EDITION.   PRICE THREE SHILLINGS AND SIXPENCE.

LONDON:

Field & Tuer, yᵉ Leadenhalle Preffe, E.C.

FIELD & TUER

YE LEADENHALLE PRESSE, E.C.

T2,88a

To Sir Henry Taylor, K.C.M.G.,

AUTHOR OF *Philip Van Artevelde.*

HEARING you speak of the literature and the literary men of the last generation—of Wordsworth whom you were one of the earliest to recognize, of Southey whom you loved, of Walter Savage Landor, and of many more, I have asked myself whether, rising up among us now, there are those who can fill their vacant place; and I have feared that the literature of to-day may seem to you less noble and less sound than that of a half-century ago. Journalism, a fleeting and sometimes flippant phase of letters, has developed since then with a speed which almost justifies Lamartine's prediction that our literature will soon consist of the daily newspaper alone. And therefore it is that I venture, in a volume compiled for the use of literary beginners, to invoke a name which will remind them of the dignity and duty of their mission.

Preface.

JOURNALISM, while it affords scope for the most brilliant and practised powers, is also the legitimate sphere for the literary beginner. His capacity is there put to the test by a process which, unlike that of publishing a book, costs him nothing in case of failure; while the acceptance of his contributions is an earnest of his future success. Nearly all our great writers, whether journalists or not, began by contributing timorously and obscurely to the newspaper and periodical press; and that there are thousands of aspirants to-day eager to follow in

their footsteps and to take a place in the Republic of
Letters, if they only knew how and where to make
a start, is the conviction which has led to the compilation of this little book. Nor is it published
without a hope that among their number may be
found in embryo the George Salas, the Tom Taylors,
the Edmund Yates,—perhaps even the Macaulays
and the George Eliots of the future.

A first edition of one thousand copies having
been exhausted in two months, the author has, in
this second issue, taken advantage of many useful
hints offered by critics, and has corrected down to
date the dictionary of the periodical press.

Contents.

"If a man can command a table, a chair, pen, ink, and paper, he can commence his trade as a literary man. It requires no capital, no special education, and may be taken up without a moment's delay."—*Anthony Trollope.*

"When my first effusion—dropped stealthily one evening at twilight, with fear and trembling, in a dark letter-box, in a dark office up a dark court in Fleet Street—appeared in the glory of print, I walked down to Westminster Hall, and turned into it for half-an-hour, because my eyes were so dimmed with joy and pride that they could not bear the street, and were not fit to be seen there."—*Charles Dickens.*

JOURNALS AND JOURNALISM.

LITERARY AMATEURS.

MATEURITY generally means immaturity. In literature it is a want of that ease, that self-possession of style, and that conformity to custom which can hardly exist without practice, and for the absence of which even freshness or impulse of manner makes poor amends. A literary aspirant, therefore, in forwarding his tentative contributions, should never apologetically explain that he is an amateur, for by so doing he will hardly fail to prejudice editors against his MSS. Let him beware also of the little dilettante habits which, though they seem to him attractive refinements, only raise a smile in Fleet-street. Such, for instance, is the good note-paper bearing a crest in the corner, commonly implying an expenditure impossible to the man who writes well enough to write for his bread. The

professional journalist "slings ink " on whatever odds and ends of paper come in his way ; and the amateur would do well to show the same wholesome indifference to the niceties of note-paper, even following, if need be, the example of "paper-sparing Pope," who wrote his "Iliad" and "Odyssey" on the backs of letters from his friends, among whom were Addison and Steele, those great fathers of literary journalism.

Even more fatally amateurish is the practice, not uncommon with beginners, of addressing a more or less gushing note to an editor, disclaiming any wish for remuneration, and intimating that the honour of appearing in his valuable paper is all the reward that is asked.   A contribution that is worth printing is worth paying for; and to an established paper the trifling sum due for any ordinary article is a matter of no consequence whatever—a mere drop in the bucket of printing and editorial expenses.   In the case of a new paper, not backed by much capital, it is different. Gratuitous contributions may there be welcome ; but such a paper will hardly live ; nor, if it did, would there be much prestige attached to an appearance in its pages. Besides, the offer of unremunerated labour to an experienced editor will often, and legitimately, be resented. He feels that an attempt is being made to bribe him, and, however absurd the bribe, the idea is not pleasant. There is, in a word, only one fair and sufficient test of capacity in literature as in the other arts, and that is the test of competition in the open market.

Our old friends, supply and demand, expressed by sale and purchase, are the only trustworthy umpires in the matter, after all.

As to the style of amateurs, though we have just spoken of freshness as their possible characteristic, the curious fact is that, contrary to natural expectation, they generally write more conventionally than the hacks of journalism. The amateur sets himself too energetically to keep the trodden ways; he is too timid to allow any originality which he may possess to assert itself; and it is only when he is familiar with the necessary laws that he gives himself a desirable ease and liberty in non-essentials. The same rule holds good with the literary novice as with the amateur actors, who, while they break the law which directs them to face their audience, are more stagy in delivery than the third-rate ranter of twenty years' experience.

Finally, let amateurs beware of "amateur magazines," and of agencies for the profitable placing of literary work. These are generally bubbles—bubbles that will burst as soon as they are pricked with a silver or a golden pin. Some years ago an action was brought by one of these amateur associations against another; and a number of dreadful young men of nineteen, with long hair, and spectacles, appeared in court as plaintiffs and defendants. No doubt the original promoters of such an organization traded to good purpose on the credulity and ambition of the provincial and the young, beginning with a profession of philanthropy, and ending with a request for a subscription.   They soon had their imitators, however; the monopoly was broken, the spoils divided; and what with the exposure resulting from their internal dissensions, and the bitter individual experience of the thousands who lent willing ears and purses to their allurements, we may hope that their occupation is now gone.

INTRODUCTIONS TO EDITORS.

THERE is an impression universally prevalent among beginners that to be introduced personally or by letter to an editor is one of the essentials of a literary *début*, albeit the only introduction which really avails is good and marketable work. It is difficult to convince them of the fact that recommendation will not do a great deal for them, or that they can possibly receive justice without it. "A good word from a trustworthy source will induce the editors to read my things," says the amateur invariably; "as it is, I am certain they do not read them." The unpalatable fact is, however, that when a MS. is not read, the reason in eight cases out of ten is that the editorial eye, which is as practised in gauging at a glance the quality of literary work as is the eye of an art collector in determining instantly the approximate value of a picture, has summarily given a decision adverse to the offered contribution. Good things are too well worth having to be carelessly foregone. Of course there are exceptions. Press of time, press of matter, or kindred

reasons, may cause a contribution to be overlooked; but in such cases a letter of introduction hardly mends matters. A familiar source of trouble to authors and professional journalists would once for all be stopped if beginners would frankly enter the field in the way of business, *sans phrases.* Of course there are cases in which a word from a common acquaintance may be of use to an unknown writer who sends to a journal an article which might possibly be a hoax; for a note of introduction is, if nothing else, a valuable guarantee of good faith. Also a letter *from one journalist to another,* vouching for the tried capacity of a person introduced, is, it is scarcely necessary to say, very useful and very convenient; it may save the time and trouble which would otherwise be spent on reading his MSS., and all editors are glad to escape at once to the plain-sailing of print; for, as Charles Lamb found, everything reads "raw" in MS. The printed copy will not necessarily be accepted, of course, but it will stand a better chance in that condition. Such an introduction as this, however, is hardly likely to fall to the lot of the beginner for whose behoof we are writing, and whom we wish to warn against counting on any kind of personal favour from an editor through common acquaintances or otherwise.

Still more futile than suing outsiders for recommendations is the somewhat kindred practice of appealing to the editor himself *in formâ pauperis,* and for personal motives, for a place upon his staff. Charles Dickens, speaking from a full heart, somewhere mentions the "profoundly unreasonable grounds on which an editor is often urged to accept unsuitable articles—such as having been at school with the writer's husband's brother-in-law, or having lent an alpenstock in Switzerland to the writer's wife's nephew, when that interesting stranger had broken his own." Thackeray resigned the editorship of the *Cornhill* (his pet magazine, set on foot at a time when monthlies of its class were few) on account of the pain he endured from the inevitable necessity of rejecting appeals, not less unreasonable and far more pitiful than the fantastic pleas caricatured by Dickens. Pathetic letters from educated young women, on whose painful exertions as teachers, and even as sempstresses, a paralyzed father or a brood of helpless younger children depended, timid supplications from men whose spirit was broken by failure in every direction— such were among the "thorns," as he called them, which the tender-hearted humourist found in the editorial pillow. Unfortunately, angelic filial or sisterly devotion is not inconsistent with the feeblest literary powers; nevertheless, the editor, hoping against hope, was wont to look eagerly through the poor little paper, in case, by some untoward chance, it might be just possible to print it—but almost always with the same negative result.* It

---

* Mr. Thackeray tells us thus much, but he does not add that he frequently sent out of his own pocket a five-pound note in payment for the contributions

is difficult for distress to be very logical, but it is also difficult to enter into the state of mind of a poor girl who thinks that her MSS. ought to be printed because *she* is good, self-denying, unfortunate and overworked, and not at all because *they* deserve it.

This sort of personal appeal is essentially feminine. So is the occasional trick of addressing contributions to the editor's private house instead of to the office of his paper. Few women are content to be numbered in a class; they will not submit to be generalized; they find some good reason why their own case is peculiar and particular; hence they pursue an editor to his home in the hope of getting his private ear, and by so doing irretrievably damage such chance of success as they might otherwise have. Those women (and they are not a few) who have made a worthy position in periodical literature, have done so by ridding themselves of all such feminine amateurity as this. Harriet Martineau, Mrs. Lynn Linton, Mrs. Cashel Hoey, these are

---

which he could neither publish nor conscientiously charge to his employers. The kind - hearted editor, whose "cynicism," by the way, is the stock charge against his character, put the impracticable MSS. away in a drawer devoted to matter destined for possible future use, where they were of course forgotten.

names with which no such petti-
fogging devices are associated.
And the story of Adelaide Anne
Procter's connection with *House-
hold Words* illustrates our point. This is how it is told by Charles
Dickens :—" In the spring of the year 1853, I observed, as conductor of *Household Words*, a short poem among the proffered contributions, very different, as I thought, from the shoal of verses per-
petually setting through the office of such a periodical, and possessing
much more merit. Its authoress was quite unknown to me. She
was one Miss Mary Berwick, whom I had never heard of; and she
was to be addressed by letter, if addressed at all, at a circulating
library in the western district of London. Through this channel
Miss Berwick was informed that her poem was accepted, and was
invited to send another. · She complied, and became a regular
and frequent contributor. Many letters passed between the journal
and Miss Berwick, but Miss Berwick herself was never seen. . . .
This went on until December, 1854, when the Christmas Number,
entitled *The Seven Poor Travellers*, was sent to press. Happen-
ing to be going to dine that day with an old and dear friend,
distinguished in literature as 'Barry Cornwall,' I took with me
an early proof of that number, and remarked, as I laid it on the
drawing-room table, that it contained a very pretty poem, written
by a certain Miss Berwick. Next day brought me the disclosure

that I had so spoken of the poem to the mother of its writer, in its writer's presence; that I had no such correspondent in existence as Miss Berwick; and that the name had been assumed by ' Barry Cornwall's ' eldest daughter, Miss Adelaide Anne Procter. This anecdote," continues Mr. Dickens, "strikingly illustrates the honesty, independence, and quiet dignity of the lady's character. I had known her when she was very young; I had been honoured with her father's friendship when I was myself a young aspirant; and she had said at home, 'If I send him in my own name verses that he does not honestly like, either it will be very painful to him to return them, or he will print them for papa's sake, and not for their own.' "

We do not say, then, that an introduction based on its writer's knowledge of the bearer's personal worth is never to be used— only that it will not avail unless along with the personal worth there is also professional skill. Nor is there any objection to a practice of addressing "copy" to an editor by name; for he may take as a compliment, to be rewarded perhaps by a careful consideration of the MS., this recognition of his individuality—a recognition which is not an offensively intrusive one. But we do warn all beginners against attempts to bring personal influence up the editorial back-stairs, instead of taking their chance fairly and frankly with the great army of unknown volunteers.

HOW TO BEGIN.

HE main difficulty in journalism, as in so many of the affairs of life, is the start. The very uncertainty of the final acceptance and success of contributions doubly disinclines the unenterprising man for the effort—often a supreme effort—of composition. Many great writers have put off unsheathing the pen as long as they could possibly afford to be idle. If Thackeray had not lost in two years the fortune he inherited when he came of age, he would probably not have become first a contributor to the press, and then the author of "Vanity Fair"; nor did the stimulus of success ever conquer his incurable dislike for steady work. A practised journalist will often confess to an utter incapacity to produce copy except under pressure of necessity. If he has a week for his task, he makes no progress . until the last days. If he has a day for it, the morning and afternoon go, and though he sits over his paper and ink, nothing is done; but at night, when the minutes left to him for the fulfilment of his engagement are precious, he gets into full swing, and

writes both rapidly and well. In short, the knowledge that the
printers are waiting for his copy is not uncommonly the only
source of the journalist's inspiration.   Mere dislike, then, for the
mental and manual labour in the production of copy need not be
taken by the literary beginner to belie his aspirations, and will
not necessarily interfere with his final success.

But obviously it is well to lessen this reluctance as far as possible.
And this can often be done by observing a rule which, on other
grounds, must be always before the eyes of the novice, viz., to
be himself in all he writes.   Longfellow's advice to the sculptor,

> " That is best which lieth nearest ;
> Shape from that thy work of art,".

is equally applicable to him.   Individuality, where it is not
eccentric, ill-timed, or out of taste, is a precious quality in an
author.   Of course he must not ride his veriest hobbies (though
they are better than commonplaces) ; but without going to ex-
tremes he ought to show in all that he writes that *he* writes it ;
and thus he will rouse the double interest of the work and of its
author in his readers.   Of course, reporting in one form and
another is a leading feature of journalism, and is an art in itself ;
and in ordinary reporting—not in special reporting, such as some of
Mr. Sala's, where no one would wish to forego the touches he gives
us of himself—it is well to lose sight of the reporters.   By them,

indeed, impersonality must be cultivated as carefully as it ought to be avoided by those whose work is of a less conventional order.

Supposing that a beginner has followed us thus far in what we have written, has studied and kept the commandments which are appended at the end of the book, has actually taken up his pen, and written something because he feels it and wants to say it ; the next step, now to be considered, is to forward the MS. to a publication into the scope of which it comes, with or without an introduction, and with or without an accompanying explanatory letter, subject to the necessities of the case, and in accordance with the hints thrown out in a past chapter. Presumably every young aspirant has his favourite newspaper, and his pet magazine ; and on the model of the writings that appear in these, he is almost sure at the outset, unless he have rare originality, to mould his own. Two other things are almost equally certain: that he will send his first-fruits to the editor whose pages have indirectly produced them; and secondly, that these first-fruits will have the blemishes which always mark imitative art, and be condemned accordingly. If under these circumstances the young author, in the bitterness of his disappointment, tear up the MS. which has been courteously returned to him, no great harm will be done. The destroying stage is one through which all must pass, even the greatest; indeed, great authors often regret they have not burned more than they did, as may be seen from the efforts of Tennyson and Mrs. Browning to suppress poems published even after they were out of their teens; while Macaulay in his full maturity could not find a market' for everything he wrote, and there are MSS. of his, according to a recent article in *Belgravia,* which still remain unpublished, and which have been spared the flames to no other purpose than to show that even a Titan's pen is sometimes wielded in vain.

But if the young author is tender about his first tentative. writing, and feels that it would be sweet to see it in print, even though "there's nothing in 't," let him venture it again, in perhaps a less ambitious quarter than before.   For, above all things, let him never be ashamed of humble beginnings.   The most unpretentious papers—even some of the cheap organs, not supposed to be read by cultivated people—have been the nurseries of fair contemporary reputations among novelists.   The literary annals of the past abound with instances of the obscure commencement of a literary career of distinction.   Nearly half-a-century has elapsed since Dickens's first effusion was "dropped stealthily, with fear and trembling, into a dark letter-box, in a dark office, up a court in Fleet Street;" and when it appeared "in all the glory of print," his sensation of pleasure was the only remuneration he expected or got.   "On that occasion," he says, "I walked down to Westminster Hall, and turned into it for half-an-hour, because my eyes were so dimmed with joy and pride that they could not bear the street, and were not fit to be seen there."   Other and more substantial recompense he had none; and before he broke his connection with the *Old Monthly Magazine,* he modestly wrote to the editor intimating that, as he had hitherto sent all his contributions gratuitously, he would now be glad if the "sketches" were thought worthy of any small remuneration, otherwise he would be obliged to discontinue them, as he was going to get married, and thus incur additional domestic expense.

Thackeray's first literary work is lost in the forgotten pages of the *Constitutional.* John Ruskin's first editor was—a clerk in the Crown Life Office! in whose *Friendship's Offering* the great art critic wrote verses at fifteen.

The distinguished author of *Self-Help* made his maiden appearance in the *Edinburgh Weekly Chronicle* (now dead), and had, a little later, very practical journalistic experience as editor of the *Leeds Times.* Hepworth Dixon began a literary career of great profit and some honour, by contributions to the obscure local press, indited from the desk of a merchant's office; and he subsequently served a hard apprenticeship to letters as editor of a Cheltenham paper. There are hundreds of similar cases among living writers.

All this should impress on the beginner that he must be humble at the outset. And with this humility, there must also be great diligence. Manuscripts must be sent from editor to editor; if they are refused by one, they will sometimes be accepted by another. Persistence is the secret of success; it is wearying work, no doubt; but how often crowned with triumph will be shown in the chapter entitled "Declined with Thanks." If all refuse them, fresh MSS. must be put in circulation, one after another in succession, until some have found a satisfactory destination, and these latter will probably help the others to obtain one too. This is a common way of getting a footing in periodical literature, and one which we have heard perhaps the most experienced editor in London recommend to young men who came to him for counsel. Another way is to take an inferior post on the literary staff of a daily paper, turning the hand to all the odds and ends of sub-editing and general reporting, and thus gradually qualifying for a more responsible position. Another and most inviting entrance into the republic of letters is that of short-hand reporting. This offers the advantage of a certain income, the enjoyment of which gives a man opportunity to turn round and see what his literary capacity is; and if that capacity stand him in good stead, he can combine its exercise with his duties in the gallery of the House of Commons, or wherever they may be; if it do not, he has a staff to lean on that is not

only a walking-stick, but a crutch. Charles Dickens, as everyone knows, began life as a re-
porter. So did Justin Mc
Carthy, M.P.; and so did many
others who now fill prominent
journalistic places. The boy, therefore, who desires to embrace
the literary calling, can prepare himself for it as soon as he is
in his teens, by learning stenography; and when the time comes
for him to make a serious choice of a profession, he will find that
the conventionally interposing parent, who, having the vision of
Chatterton's suicide and Johnson's poverty always before him,
would not allow his son to trust to literature as a means of
subsistence, will offer no objection to his practising reporting—a
lucrative and steady career. And once in communication with the
world of editors and journalists, the young short-hand writer will
soon feel his way to whatever he is fit for in literary labour. Again,
a few beginners have first accepted posts in the commercial
department of a newspaper office, and, having come so near
to the editorial sanctum, at last enter it, relinquishing their
mechanical work as they are able to get other that is more to
their minds. This preliminary desk-work is drudgery, no doubt,
just as it was in a lawyer's office to young Disraeli and to
Lever; so also is reporting; but those who undertake these
duties often do so to meet manfully and legitimately the natural

B

wishes of parents, who, as old Isaac Disraeli says, see in the son who opposes them in the choice of a calling, and whom posterity may recognize as a genius, only the wilful and rebellious child. And, indeed, by the endurance of this drudgery young aspirants show of what metal they are made, and prove that they have confidence in themselves and in their true vocation—a confidence which, when it has stood so practical a test, rarely turns out to be misplaced. Other employments than those which we have named, connected with the production of a journal, may sometimes be the preparatory stages of a literary career, but are not of a nature that would lead us to recommend their adoption to that end. The "reader," who cudgels his brains over the "proofs" of what others have written, occasionally begins to write himself. Even the printer has been known to make his way into the editor's or author's chair, and to fill it with credit — seldomer, perhaps, in England, where Douglas Jerrold was among the number, than in America, where Franklin, Horace Greeley, Bennett, Bret Harte, and Artemus Ward, with many others only less renowned, once stood at the compositor's case.

DECLINED WITH THANKS.

NO consolations that we can here offer will be able to mitigate the sting of a first—or, indeed, of a second or of a third—reception of this courteous but inexorable form of refusal. It is not until after one or two acceptances of MS. that a rejection becomes in any degree tolerable. When the acceptances outnumber the rejections, indeed, "Declined with thanks" will generally cease to cause a serious pang. At that happy time, too, it will matter little to an author whether his refusal come to him in these laconic words, or in the longer forms which are designed to save his sensitiveness by a vague suggestion of some rather unusual reason for the return of good work. But to the novice the form really makes some difference ; to hear that his copy is "not suitable" for the pages of this or that paper gives him the comforting reflection that he has in some way failed to hit the editor's individual taste, or that his subject is considered to be one that could be more appropriately treated elsewhere. Still more gently is he soothed if his pill come to him gilded with an intimation that an unusual press of matter has prevented the appearance in print of his contribution. The following note illustrates this more tender editorial mood :—

"The editor of the *Contemporary Review* is much obliged by Mr. ———'s offer of his paper. It is too able an article not to have been read with interest, but the editor regrets to say that it is quite impracticable to find room for the topic. In reforwarding the MS. by this book-post, the editor begs to add his best thanks."

If the author accepts such little comforts resignedly, so much the better. But so much the worse—very much indeed the worse —if, being of a too persevering or persistent disposition, he should argue the point with the well-meaning editor. Let him at all events accept as final a refusal for which he may find any reason that consoles him most; to dispute the justice of the verdict, or even to offer to alter, tone down, or improve the MS. with a view to obtaining a more favourable resolution, is only to involve a busy editor in an irritating waste of time, and to gradually discourage the use of polite forms and, indeed, the return of rejected MSS. at all. An unsuccessful author is really to be pitied if the work of some months of thought and some days or weeks of laborious penmanship finds its ignominious way into the editorial wastepaper basket—a fate which, to the great credit of editors generally, very rarely befalls it, and this in spite of the dismal warnings which are printed at the beginning or end of most periodicals to the effect that unsuitable MSS. will never be returned. In view of such ill-fortune at any time occurring to him, the beginner would do well, in the case of serious and laborious work, to make duplicates of his compositions by means of one or other of the cheap and easily-worked contrivances for multiplying impressions; unless, indeed, as is likely to be the case, he has rough drafts, scored with corrections, of the finally-approved MS. ready at hand to work upon again. The more there are of these rough drafts the better will it be, and the less likely that the writer will need to go to them again; for well has it been said—and this must be impressed on the amateur's mind—that "the men who have the fewest MSS. returned are the men who have taken the greatest pains with their work." Macaulay and Cardinal Newman penned many of their pages twice, thrice, and oftener; George Henry Lewes, after having an article returned from the *Edinburgh*, thenceforth re-wrote everything before submitting it to a magazine; while in journalism Mr. Albany Fonblanque, we are told by his nephew, Mr. Edward Barrington de Fonblanque, "frequently wrote an article ten times over before it contented him, and even then he very rarely read it after publication without wishing to re-write it." When, indeed, such articles as these, or when poems and stories, which after a few weeks or months of reflection do not appear to be immature to the authors themselves, are returned, let them not be committed to the flames. At some future date they will serve the writer's purpose; especially if in the meantime he. has made a success by some other effort. Thackeray's earlier compositions, both in prose and verse, which either "the leading magazines had all refused to print" or the public had refused to read, were all blazoned years afterwards in the pages of the *Cornhill;* Nathaniel Hawthorne had a similar experience in the new world; and we have heard the editor who, if we remember right, introduced "East Lynne" to the world, say that Mrs. Henry Wood had at the time of that first success a drawer full of tales which had been "returned with thanks" from all directions, but which were afterwards printed, handsomely paid for, and duly admired. Of course these are exceptional cases; and it will be better and wiser, as a rule, for the beginner to allow the fugitive literary attempts, of which he himself may feel somewhat uncertain, to take their chance, sink or swim, survive or die, as fortune may immediately decide.

Stinging and discouraging and incapacitating as a "Declined with thanks" may seem to the novice who for the first time tears open the heartless packet which discloses to him the characters of his own familiar hand, there is a solid and abundant consolation for him—as regards his hopes of ultimate success, at least—in the long roll of precedent. The failures of men destined to be great do not date from yesterday. Editors and publishers have declined with thanks—and without them—the masterpieces of the world. The ill-fortune of "Paradise Lost" is almost too hackneyed an example to quote; but perhaps everyone does not know, or does not remember, that "Robinson Crusoe," which, were it ever by possibility out of print, would be a European loss, went begging through the circle of English publishers, until one, more speculative but generally considered less discriminating than the rest, consented to print the immortal book and to pocket a thousand guineas at once by his venture. It is scarcely necessary to say that "Robinson Crusoe" is one of the staple sources of profit to a thousand publishers, and holds its own in spite of the innumerable desert islands which have studded the oceans of juvenile fiction since the first appeared. And this almost unanimous refusal encountered Defoe's attempt, not when he was young and unknown, but after the establishment of his repute as a writer. And to come to later examples, everyone knows how the author of "Jane Eyre" wrote a novel in friendly competition with her two sisters (the story is admirably told by Charlotte Brontë herself in the pathetic introduction she wrote for an edition of Emily Brontë's *Wuthering Heights*), and how it went a weary round of publishers, declined with thanks by each alike, but every time courageously despatched on its travels again by the indomitable little Yorkshire governess until the signs (frankly unconcealed) of so many rejections awoke some kindly interest, on the part of Messrs. Smith and Elder's critic, in the battered MS. and its persistent author. Thackeray, Charlotte Brontë's contemporary and friend, failed, and failed repeatedly, not only at drawing, which he did badly, but at writing, which he did eminently well, for his contributions, as we have already said, were at first refused by all the leading magazines. Carlyle, after being "edited" out of all recognition in the *Edinburgh Review*, was finally rejected as a contributor altogether. Mr. Kinglake's "Eöthen," though composed with thought, and the work of years, scrupulously revised, and, in fact, fulfilling the Horatian maxim of delay, was utterly, unconditionally, and irrevocably rejected by every publisher to whom the author offered it. At last he found one who would consent to accept the precious and classic little work as a present, judging it just worthy of printer's ink and paper. Nor did "Eöthen," after this disheartening beginning, instantaneously burst into popularity like "Robinson Crusoe." At first it seemed that the publishers were right, and that it would remain a failure to the end; but the event has brought a very different verdict. Anthony

Trollope, in his middle age the most read, as he is perhaps the most readable, of novelists, was fain in early life to taste the bitterness of rejection not once or twice; the judicious, easy, and always refined pen which has now a fortune at command, gained an income of £12 5s. 7½d. in one of the first years of its labours, and of £20 2s. 6d. in another. Hepworth Dixon experienced no small difficulty in finding a publisher for his "Memoir of Howard," which, when it was at last issued, went through three editions within a year. The great American historian, Motley, had his "Dutch Republic" returned with thanks; a similar fate befell Carlyle's "French Revolution;" and Lingard's history, which every year commands more attention and esteem, also shared the doom of refusal. Lord Brougham was rejected; Jeffrey, the rejector, was rejected; George Eliot herself is said to have been rejected until she found a masculine advocate in George Henry Lewes; but George Henry Lewes was rejected! Indeed, it is easier to say who has *not*, than who *has*, undergone that blank moment of chilled and disappointed hope—our readers' experience of which will, we trust, be limited.

And to this end, let it be always remembered that the tact which produces *marketable* work is sometimes more useful than the talent which produces *good* work. Unhappily, the two things are not always identical. A composition of real power and originality may in fact, and not merely in the terms of editorial courtesy, be

unsaleable because it is unjournalistic in manner or inopportune
to the time. This fact should not fail to soften disappointments.
And furthermore, if a rejected beginner should be tempted
to indulge the frame of mind most fatal to all his chances of
success—a conviction of personal injury—he should restore a
healthy tone to his mind by believing, what is the truth, that
editors are kind, through a fellow-feeling and a remembrance of
their own apprenticeship ; and just, through a fair consideration of
self-interest. Let him reflect for a moment on the number of
newspapers, reviews, and magazines which are produced daily,
weekly, and monthly in England, and on the number of pens at
work upon only one issue of one of these, and he will easily
perceive that the competition for securing good contributions is
very keen and very busy. "Returned with thanks," is not likely
to be written without a reason. When, therefore, publishers and
editors have fallen into real mistakes, as in the famous instances
we have cited, allowance must simply be made for their fallibility
as men who have to gauge the taste of a whimsical and often
irrational public, and who sometimes gauge it wrong. No one
could foretell with certainty that "Jane Eyre" would take the
country as it did ; and in Thackeray's case it was no editorial
caprice which condemned him to a period of obscurity, for the
public at first altogether failed to taste the peculiar flavour of his
genius, thus in a manner justifying the rejection : for an editor's

office is not to defy, but half to guide and half to wait upon, the public. "So your poor Titmarsh has made another fiasco," wrote Thackeray, when a little volume of his failed. "How are we to take this great stupid public by the ears? Never mind; I think I have something which will surprise them yet." The "something" proved to be "Vanity Fair;" and the "great stupid public" whose good word he was too wise to underrate even while he smiled at its slowness, awoke to the full knowledge of one more great author, and will never forget him.

But what we have said would fail of half its purpose were it only to offer a balm to the wounds of the young author whose MS. has been returned or silently consigned to the editorial waste-paper basket. It is also intended to inculcate industry, perseverance, and a courage that does not flag because the first effort, or the fifth, is a failure. "We should certainly shrink," says the *Saturday Review*, cynical in the consciousness that it possesses an adequate staff of its own, "from the responsibility of recommending perseverance to the writers of rejected MSS.; but," and this is the part of the paragraph which it is to our point to quote here, "we cannot deny that unflinching perseverance sometimes succeeds at last." Instead of "sometimes" we should be inclined to use a more encouraging word, because we are convinced that among the aspirants for literary honours the minority, and not the majority, are incapable. Of course, worthless writing will gain nothing by the persistence of the writer; but the best authors our literature has known would, without persistence, have failed to obtain for their genius that recognition which is its very life.

POUNDS, SHILLINGS, AND PENCE.

GOOD deal has happened since Charles Lamb wrote paragraphs for sixpence apiece in the *Morning Post;* though it must not be forgotten that the age of pence has given place to an age of shillings, not only in literature, but in everything else ; and the paragraphists of to-day's *Pall Mall,* who get about sixpence for a single line, spend that sixpence with an ease to which, fifty years ago, they would have been strangers. Bearing this in mind, the case of Southey may be taken as typical, not so much of the active journalist as of the reviewer and essayist, both of that and of this day ; and it is not a comfortable one to contemplate. "Prose," writes Sir Henry Taylor of his friend, "having been almost the only resource of one who was at once an eminent poet, and in general literature the most distinguished writer of his age (Mr. Southey), his example may be fairly adduced as showing what can be made of it under the most favourable circumstances. By a small pension and the office of Laureate (yielding together

about £200 per annum) he was enabled to insure his life to make a moderate posthumous provision for his family ; and it remained for him to support himself and them, so long as he should live, by his writings.　With unrivalled industry, infinite stores of knowledge, extraordinary talents, a delightful style, and the devotion of about one-half of his time to writing what should be marketable rather than what he would have desired to write, he defrayed the cost of that frugal and homely way of life which he deemed to be the happiest and the best.　But at sixty years of age he had never yet had one year's income in advance, and when between sixty and seventy his powers of writing failed, had it not been for the timely grant of an additional pension his means of subsistence would have failed too."　We have spoken of this as a typical case, yet it is hardly so except in its disheartening pecuniary results, for in its conditions it was made more than typically favourable by Southey's ability, his pension, his connexions, and his quite enormous industry.　In saying that these results represent literary rewards, not only in that day, but in our own, we make a statement to which Mr. James Payn—who recently contributed to the *Nineteenth Century* a bright article which, if he will permit us to say so, never allows us to forget that its author is a writer of romance— will doubtless demur.　"Poor Paterfamilias," he says, "looking hopelessly about him, like Quintus Curtius in the riddle, for a nice opening for a young man, is totally ignorant of the opportunities, if not for fame and fortune, at least for competency and comfort, that literature now offers to a clever lad. He believes, perhaps, that it is only geniuses that succeed in it; or, as is more probable, he regards it as a hand-to-mouth calling, which to-day gives its disciples a five-pound note and to-morrow five pence. He calls to mind a saying about literature being a good stick, but not a good crutch—an excellent auxiliary, but no permanent support; but he forgets the all-important fact that the remark was made half-a-century ago." This is all very well from that most fortunate of literary men, a clever and successful novelist, who shines in a sphere of the profession which cannot well at any time be overcrowded. He, clearly, is not in a position to judge either for the average essayist or for the journalist proper.

And here let us pause a moment to make a necessary distinction between two divisions of the profession we are considering, literature and journalism—taking literature to mean broadly the writing of books, magazines, and reviews, and journalism the writing for newspapers. These are distinct in the talents, character, aims, and remunerations which they imply. A journalist is bound to be a man of the world, as an author is bound to be a student. The former developes a capacity for representing his era, for letting the general opinion speak through him even while he helps to guide it. He produces work which is eminently marketable; and the more of this quality appears in his writings, the more

G. A. Sala.

successful he will be. Mr. Sala is a king among journalists; his success is pre-eminent, proverbial; yet it is said that he is wont to tell his friends that he took to journalism because he failed, only comparatively, of course, in literature. That there are differences in the requisite talents, therefore, is clear. Not a few are able to combine the two things, to be at once students and men of the world, but in these instances journalism generally is subservient to authorship, or *vice versâ*, according to the state of the author's mind or of his finances—for these two branches of the profession differ, as we have said, not only in the qualifications they require, but also in the scale of their rewards.

Southey, of course, belonged to literature; and we shall first consider what work of the same order as his, which was wretchedly paid then, is valued at in the market now. Fiction we leave out of the question; the price it fetches is far in excess of that which is given for prose writing of any other kind, and is magnificent. And this, whatever may be said, was the case half-a-century ago as it is now—was so when Walter Scott annually made £10,000 for several years, quite as much as when George Eliot received for " Romola " £8,000. Other literary labour cuts a sorry figure in comparison. Were not Mr. Payn, who probably commands his fifty shillings a page for

fiction, a writer of novels, he
would give a less seductive
view of the profits of the
literary career. For the pound
which the *Nineteenth Century*, and the *Contemporary*, and the
Quarterly pay for a printed page is quite the highest regulation
rate of remuneration for the periodical essayist and reviewer.
The shilling monthlies give *on an average* rather under than over
half that sum; while in a certain high-class weekly, a long book-
notice, which has, perhaps, involved the patient study of two
bulky volumes, and which, when done conscientiously, has
consumed some five or six days, has only £2 as its pecuniary
equivalent. Another literary weekly, where, again, the work
involves the twofold task of reading and writing, pays 10s. a
column; and other papers, of less eminence, in proportion.
This might be very fair remuneration were not work of the
kind difficult to get, and doled out in minute portions, week
by week, month by month, quarter by quarter. The magazines,
reviews, and literary papers of standing can almost be counted on
the fingers; and with an army of applicants for an appearance in
their pages, no one man, however brilliant he may be, can have
anything like a monopoly. Perhaps hardly a single writer on
any of the weekly literary papers has an article inserted every
week throughout the year; yet, if he had, his total earnings would

only amount to a sum which it would be a mockery to speak of, in the ordinary sense, as an income. Do the monthly magazines offer better rewards? If in one or other of them a single writer made one monthly appearance (and what a brilliant writer he would be!), the result would certainly be less than £150 per annum; yet the amateur, seeing that writer's name in the *Cornhill* one month, in *Macmillan* the next, in *The Contemporary* the month after, would, perhaps, imagine him to be rolling in wealth. It is hardly a secret that even Mr. Mallock, who not only writes well, but has caught the public ear, and whose work is welcomed by *The Nineteenth Century*, *The Contemporary*, and *The Edinburgh*, has hitherto made an income by his pen quite insufficient to allow him to regard literature as his career.

Poetry, like fiction, is exceptional; the former being, in a general way, as much less, as the latter is more, remunerative than other literary work. Of course the public has its one prime poetical favourite, and pays him well, though not better now (as Mr. Tennyson would feelingly assure Mr. Payn) than it did fifty years ago. Until last year the Laureate received, from one firm, annually £4,000 for his copyrights; but there is only room for one Tennyson at a time. Walter Scott got 2,000 guineas for the "Lady of the Lake," but Walter Scott had to abandon poetry as soon as Lord Byron appeared; and while Lord Byron was calculating one morning that he had made £24,000 by poetry,

Shelley was complaining of the printer's bill he had to defray
out of his own pocket. Poetry like Southey's paid little in that
day, and would pay less now. Mr. Browning's receipts may be
smaller than those of some of the veriest hacks in prose.
Mr. Edwin Arnold would probably get more for a dozen political
leaders, hastily thrown off, than for the " Light of Asia," a work
of scholarly erudition, of inspired poetry, and the outcome of
half a lifetime of Oriental study and sympathy—a work which has
fixed his place among the English bards. And Mr. Aubrey
de Vere—whom Landor loved, and whom Sir Henry Taylor
names in the same breath with Wordsworth—would probably
have to confess that his lifelong service of the muse brought him
less than his handful of articles in the *Edinburgh* years ago,
containing, in all, the prose writing of perhaps a single month.
The magazine verse of to-day is excellent, and is paid for in
the best quarters at the rate of about half-a-crown a line; in
others, two guineas, a guinea, and even half-a-guinea are the sums
given for a short set of verses. And the supply of such poetry
is, of course, largely in excess of the demand. Clearly, then, in
all these cases, literature, while an excellent stick, and one which
we would encourage amateurs to use, is decidedly unsafe as
a crutch.

But journalism can give a somewhat better account of itself.
Those arts which bring their votaries into close contact with men,

and into the full light of publicity, are usually enriched with the rewards attending effective performance. The musician who creates—the composer—is seldom fortunate in his lifetime, while the musician who performs—the singer—has the wealth of kings at his feet. This case is rather an exaggeration of that of author and journalist; still there is a resemblance: the journalist gets the ear of the public; his writing is good performance, rather than creation, for it must be not so much original as interpretative, both of public opinion and of the collected literary opinions of the world.

The work of the journalist is in constant demand; his organs infinitely outnumber the organs of literature, and they appear weekly, daily, and twice a day, instead of once a quarter, once a month, and once a week. Every daily, for instance, gives employment to a large and well-rewarded staff. There are the editor, the sub-editors, the special correspondents, the regularly retained leader-writers, most of whose salaries, in the case of the *Times*—naturally the most profitable daily to be connected with—go into four figures; nor are the other London dailies far behind the leading organ in the remuneration of their staff. The work is wearing, no doubt; but the pecuniary returns are sufficient to tempt able men to undertake it, and to make it a career which a man who has no private means, and who wishes to prosper in the world and to provide for his family, can afford deliberately to enter on. But for the dailies, destitution would stare many a journalist in the face. And not only does each maintain its established staff, which, in the case of the *Times*, is, of course, immense; but it also gives employment to a large class of journalistic irregulars, who turn their hands to anything—the unattached (sometimes by their faults, and sometimes by their misfortunes) penny-a-liners—three-halfpence-a-liners, would be nearer the mark —of the press. Always living from hand to mouth, and often on the verge of destitution, this large body of literary casuals includes in its ranks three principal classes—that of the men of brilliant powers and education, in whom the quality of sustained industry is wanting, and who might have developed into Macaulays but for this deficiency; that of the industrious, who are useful and handy, but whose capacity is mediocre; and that of the possessors of both talent and perseverance who work when and how they can, no assured position having yet fallen to their lot. That such men as these are often hungry is a fact, and one of the saddest facts of modern intellectual life. Even the new world has to tell the same story. "Two-thirds of all the working journalists of the country," says a writer in *Harper's Monthly,* "receive less than the wages of good mechanics." "I believe the majority of us," says an American journalist, Mr. A. F. Hill, "have passed through the hard-up days. What is the use of denying it? I have worked for five dollars a week, and slept on a pile of exchanges. I have seen the time when 'circumstances over which I had no control' dictated to me the necessity—not merely the propriety—of eating plainer food than I would have liked—plainer food than the kind I needed, and of not even wasting any of that. I have seen the time when a person I know very intimately has gone without food for days at a time, and that when in excellent bodily health, and blessed (?) with an unusual appetite. I have seen the days of threadbare clothes, of dilapidated shoes, and a 'shocking bad hat;' and when it brought the hot blood to my face to hear careless and happy and well-fed and well-clothed people merrily singing the chorus of a well-known song :

> " Too proud to beg, too honest to steal,
>   We know what it is to be wanting a meal ;
>   Our tatters and rags we try to conceal,
>   We belong to the ' Shabby Genteel.' "

Such experiences as these are not unknown among some of our own most painstaking journalists who seem to be fairly busy, and some of whom are, in fact, on the high road to fame. The world hears little about such poverty as this, but it is none the less real ; nay, if it were a little less so, there would be less of a sensitive desire to lock it in silence. When *The Edinburgh* was projected in Jeffrey's elevated lodging, Sydney Smith proposed as its motto, *Tenui musam meditamur avenâ* (we cultivate literature on a little oatmeal); but the phrase was not adopted, because, as a matter of fact, it came so near the truth. However, the pecuniary result of the *Edinburgh* brings us back to a brighter train of thought. The journalist sometimes rises to a position of wealth and honour, not only as an editor, but also as a newspaper proprietor. If he have the tact and talent to start a really successful journal on his own account, he comes on a pecuniary windfall; such a one, for instance, as is the *World* to Mr. Edmund Yates. This, of course, is an idyllic state of things; where the author is selling and profiting by his own wares without being preyed on unconscionably by publishers and middle-men.

But if it is comparatively rare that the functions of author and publisher can be united in one man, it is not so, as we have already hinted, in regard to the functions incidental to the two divisions of the writer's profession—literature and journalism. Many men are able to practise at once in the one and the other, and this capability lightens up some of the gloomier facts we have noted in a separate consideration of the two branches of the career. The two things work together, as nearly every writer knows. The votary of literature, in the sense in which we have used the word, may turn his hand to just so much journalism as will keep "the pot boiling;" while the journalist pleasantly and profitably stops the rapid and ephemeral exercise of his anonymous pen, to indite

something of a graver or more imaginative order to which he has
the novel satisfaction of appending his name.

The following memorandum, which has been supplied to us by
a young *littérateur,* whose experience may be taken as representative of that of a fairly successful and industrious member of his
profession, will not be without an interest for those who are about
to adopt literature as a career :—

"At the age of twenty-five, having scribbled in a purposeless,
unprofessional way for several years, I suffered a reverse of fortune
which made me exceedingly anxious to increase my diminished
private means. Literature seemed the only thing ready to hand.
I consulted two or three friends who already held more or less
prominent positions on the press, and I found that the more
successful they were the more hopeless was the prospect they held
out of my chances of making money, even in the most moderate
amounts. This I thought rather strange, but I remembered that
the author of the celebrated crutch and stick saying was Walter
Scott, who made, all the same, a gigantic fortune by his pen, and
I determined to show my discouraging advisers what I could do.
I was told that the 'Society papers' paid better than any others,
and that there was more opening on them than on the older
journals, which had already a huge literary connexion. This I
found to be the fact, and, although I tried valiantly to get a market
for serious work, it had far less acceptance than had the 'trifles

light as air' which I tossed off in other directions. I had several
introductions to editors—and they ended in nothing : my work
was my only introduction to the papers on which I got employment—a fact which I recommend to the notice of the amateurs
for whose benefit you are writing. I find that I have kept a
record of my third year's labour. I had about 200 paragraphs
in *The World;* a still greater number, and ten articles besides, in
another society paper ; thirty paragraphs in *Truth;* five articles in
The Queen; three articles in *The Spectator;* a poem in *Good
Words;* a poem in *The Quiver;* thirty-five articles in different
monthly magazines ; fifty-two columns of London correspondence
in a provincial paper (at 12s. 6d. a column); twenty-six London
letters in a Colonial paper (at 10s. a letter) ; and a few odds and
ends besides. These are the accepted contributions, but they
represent little more than half of that which I actually wrote—
the balance having missed fire. My total proceeds were
£247 13s. 2d. I often worked twelve hours a day, and I never
had a week's holiday. But, as you see, if I had not possessed a
trifle of my own, I could not have kept a decent roof over my
family's head. And yet I have often been told by other struggling
men that I am exceptionally lucky."

From this statement it will be seen that the writer had the
advantage of practice in both literature and journalism ; on the
other hand, lest the results should be unduly deterrent, let us note

c

that he had no work on a daily, nor had he any subject to treat that
was peculiarly his own. The man with a specialty, the art critic,
or the dramatic critic, for instance, if he be really proficient, has
some advantages over his more versatile brother; he may have to
compete very hard for his post, but, once having obtained it, he
has a monopoly on the particular paper with which he is connected. Moreover, he is sometimes able in a sense to duplicate
his work, as did Mr. Tom Taylor,
for instance, when he criticised
pictures in both the *Graphic* and
The Times. And who shall say
that there are no good incomes to be made on newspapers while
mentioning the name of the late editor of *Punch?*

Nor must it be forgotten that the Fleet Street journalist has
frequently, in addition to his London work, profitable employment
on a country paper. A great many leaders in the provincials are
the work of metropolitan pens; and the London correspondence
also that appears in them affords scope for a good deal of literary
labour and enterprise. Many of these journals contain excellent
personal information, which was, in fact, the natural precursor of
the society journals—these latter supplying a place which the
London dailies failed to fill. There is, no doubt, an enormous
amount of trash written in the shape of London letters and
gossip; but there is also much interesting and good matter, such

as it is natural enough that people should like to read. A few country papers have a special wire, and telegraph every night a London letter which contains "tips" usually sent in, as are the paragraphs in the society papers, not by one man, but by many. Some of these letters cost the proprietors from £1,000 to £2,000 a year. It sometimes happens—Mr. Lucy's is a case in point— that one man is able enough to take entire charge of a letter of the kind, and by manifolding it for papers in different parts of the country, can afford to do his work really well and to supply it cheaply, at the same time securing a fair income. Then, again, there is the London correspondentship for the Colonies, for the United States; and all parts of the Continent. Some of these posts are among the prizes of literature, and they fall to such men as Mr. Joseph Hatton, a knight of the pen who has fought and won in nearly every field of letters, and who is the English correspondent of the *New York Times.*

If the reader should think that our illustrations in this chapter have been somewhat conflicting, or complain that we arrive at no definite deductions, we, for our part, must own to having been met on our inquiry by many contradictions. But we shall not go far wrong, nor raise false hopes or false fears, if we sum up by saying of the incomes made by the writers in newspapers and magazines:

Sufficient, they may be ; fair, according to the infallible balance of supply and demand, they must be ; but they are seldom brilliant. There is probably bread to be had, in requital of industry and of the indispensable capacity, for all who are likely to make a serious profession of letters ; but there are few—very few—fortunes to be won.

JOURNALISM AS A CAREER.

I. The Fair Side.

IT is more effective to take the extreme uplands or lowlands of exaggeration than the *via media* of fact. Consequently those who have treated of journalism and literature as a profession have generally been tempted to strike their readers' fancy by a picturesque view of the advantages and disadvantages of a calling in which the *pros* and *cons* are in truth tolerably balanced. We all know the starving author of tradition; and if he is now somewhat out of date we have still the constant repetition of a facile and rather wearisomely conventional joke by which the labours of a labourer who is, like all others, worthy of his hire, appear as a drug in the market—witness the inevitable waste-paper basket which is thrown at his head by *Punch* and other humourists when subjects for jesting flag. There is, on the other hand, the *couleur de rose* view which has recently been asserted in one or two quarters, not,

of course, with an intention to mislead, but decidedly with the
effect of doing so, and this probably with serious consequences.
Our own task is to state advantages and disadvantages with the
single intention of making the truth stand forth, to encourage what
is now the widespread ambition of having a voice in the great
expression of public opinion, but to avoid the grave responsibility
of leading the inexperienced to cast themselves blindfold into a
career in which they may be doomed to disappointment. The fair
surface being the uppermost, we shall consider it first, and then
proceed to turn it over and to expose with all frankness the seamy
under-side.

The advantages which journalism has at first sight over all other
professions are very obvious, and may be stated in the words of
Mr. Anthony Trollope and Mr. James Payn. "It is," says the
former, "a business which has its allurements. It requires no
capital, no special education, and may be taken up at any time
without a moment's delay. If a man can command a table, a
chair, pen, ink, and paper, he can commence his trade as a literary
man. It is thus that aspirants generally do commence it."
"There are," says Mr. Payn, "hundreds of clever young men who
are now living at home and doing nothing, who might be earning
very tolerable incomes by their pens if they only knew how."
While accepting these statements as containing part-truths, it is
necessary for a moment to give them certain limitations which

modify but do not refute the contention of the two authors. We grant that it is possible for the hundreds of clever young men who are able to continue to " live at home," and who have no imperative necessity for doing something else, to make incomes which shall be eminently "tolerable" under the circumstances. Journalism on these conditions can hardly be called a career, or—what Mr. Trollope calls it—a trade. It is a part-profession, an auxiliary of more or less value and effectiveness in proportion to the cleverness possessed by the young men in question. As for the training, it is certainly not indispensable before making a first attempt; but every rejection which the young man undergoes (and he will have many to endure) is a part of his training, and a part which he would find very hard to bear if he were entirely dependent on his pen. When Mr. Anthony Trollope gives us the financial statement already quoted of the results of his first years of labour, is he not in fact describing a particularly hard period of literary noviceship—a period which *might* be full of the bitterest privations, occurring as it does at a time of life when a man is no longer enjoying the parental care and support which are cheerfully accorded to him in earlier years? That such a noviceship and preparation were tolerable, or perhaps possible, to Mr. Trollope is simply due to the fact that he held at the time a position in the

Post-office which was practically his profession, *i.e.*, his means of support, and hence that he was able to follow literature for a time as an amateur. When he talks of an aspirant "commencing his trade" with "a chair, pen, ink, and paper," his own experience might have convinced him that it is hardly a trade which is commenced with that stock, but rather a training for a trade. The same holds good with Thackeray, only that instead of a place in the Post-office he had at his back a small private fortune, the larger part of which he devoted to buying literary experience—in other words, he lost it in the attempt to float a couple of newspapers. Another novelist and journalist, Mr. Edmund Yates, was, like Mr. Anthony Trollope, in the Post-office, and thus able to exercise his "prentice hand" at letters until such time as they should yield him not only support but fortune: Mr. Wilkie Collins, another ultimately successful master of fiction, had the support of his father's help in the tea-trade first and afterwards in the law, while his literary talents were under trial. It would certainly seem, then, that technical training, with the sacrifice of time and money which it necessarily implies, is generally deferred rather than foregone; that no *special* success, at any rate, is possible without it; and that even the humbler branches of journalism can ill afford to dispense with it. No one, for instance, who has read Charles

Dickens's description of the difficulties of mastering short-hand related in the person of David Copperfield—the long study, the fever in which Traddles's declamation and "my aunt's" "hear, hear," were reported, and the impossibility of reading the report when completed—will come to the conclusion that the science of stenography, at least, needs no technical preparation.

Having made these modifications—a duty we feel bound to perform even at the expense of our point—we conceive that there remains in the modified version of the statements quoted an advantage for the beginner in literature which justifies us in even making a parade of them, and which will be missed by the beginner in almost any other career. If it has been necessary to guard the amateur against the supposition that without training, and before he is out of his teens, he can make a good and supporting income by scribbling, we must still point out that he possesses the opportunity afforded by hardly another profession, of carrying on his training and his trade at the same moment. Even supposing that for the first five years of his labour all he wrote were rejected, or printed without remuneration, he would be in no worse position than his neighbour who is articled to a solicitor but his MSS., if he has the making of a literary man in him at all, will not be treated so badly as that. Anthony Trollope's first year's real return for his literary labour was the experience he gained in it, and with only that in almost any other profession he would have had to be satisfied; but, as it was, he made a few pounds besides. Thus the literary novice may know that even while he is educating himself he can earn an income which, though it will be insufficient to maintain him except in a Grub-street garret, will at any rate contribute towards his support during a period in which he would otherwise be more likely than not to depend for that support wholly on his private resources. If Mr. Payn and Mr. Trollope had borrowed the words of a recent writer in *Belgravia*, who said, "Anyone can *scribble*—if he only knows how to spell; but writing is an art—one of the Fine Arts," and had added that even *scribbling*, if fairly clever, is remunerated after a fashion, while at the same time it trains the pen—they would perhaps have stated their case in a more strictly accurate and intelligent way. And even this text would have justified them, and justifies us, in preaching the superiority of letters over almost any other career in its beginnings.

We have already drawn a distinction between journalism and other departments of letters. The apprenticeship over and a fair success once attained, how does this branch of literature look as a career? That it is interesting, that it has the attraction of a variety of thoughts and feelings, that it brings a man into close connection with all the moving principles and large ideas of his day, is sufficient reason why it should be loved. It compares temptingly in this respect with those commercial pursuits which are becoming every day more and more the necessary callings of gentlemen. The banker must needs think money during the whole of his working day, the tea-dealer perforce thinks tea, and the wine-merchant wine ; politics, literature, social interests, science and art are with them extra-professional, if, indeed, business be not so paramount as to drive these almost entirely from the field of thought. And the liberal vocations are limited more or less to their own *spécialité ;* the artist is not called upon to know much about letters, the politician may be profoundly ignorant of painting, the *savant* generally considers himself privileged to hold politics in supreme contempt, and the musician above all is apt to dispense himself from the most ordinary interest in everything that is not musical. Now, the *littérateur* is not only encouraged but obliged to be various ; well for him ; he is so much the more a man ; and even if he choose some special "line" for the labours of his pen, if he devote the best of his powers to "knowing everything of something," he yet multiplies his resources, interests, and pleasures by "knowing something of everything."

The earnest physician holds his profession to be a noble one because it saves individual lives, but the journalist's career will give him the opportunity of saving nations by his advocacy of peace at a time when war is at once imminent and unnecessary. He is the mainstay of the reformer and of the philanthropist, who would labour in vain if unassisted by the soldier of the

pen. In a hundred instances journals have been the means
of raising large funds to meet emergencies of distress. We find
even a light paper like the Paris *Figaro* becoming the centre of
a widespread organization for the relief of indigence during a
winter of extreme severity. And an Irish priest writes from the
midst of a starving population to the correspondent of the
paper he names : " But for you and the *Daily Telegraph* I
know not how under Heaven I could have stayed famine here
To my last breath shall I remember you with undying affection and
gratitude." And in like manner, twenty years ago, *The Times's*
strenuous advocacy of the cause of English houseless poor in a
cold season resulted in a handsome sum for their relief. Scarcely
less practical a charity is that which is performed by the press
when it exposes the frauds that would gain currency did they
escape its vigilance. This is a duty which has its dangers, as was
shown for instance in 1841, when *The Times* was instrumental in
detecting a scheme organized by a company to defraud by forgery
all the influential bankers of Europe, and when an exposure in its
columns brought on the proprietors an action for libel, Boyle *v.*
Lawson, in which our law technically compelled the jury to give
a verdict for the plaintiff, with one farthing damages. A European
subscription was set on foot to reimburse the proprietors for their
immense outlay in legal expenses, but they declined the money,

and the greater portion of it was finally spent in establishing
Times scholarships for Oxford and Cambridge at Christ's Hospital
and the City of London School.   Such are some of the lofty and
humanitarian inducements to enter the profession of letters ; while
the ardent politician, if he be entrusted with the direction of an
important paper, wields, as was once said of the editor of *The
Times*, "a power as great as that of Governments and Legislatures."
Moreover, in all that he writes he has the inspiration not only of
his cause, but of knowing that he addresses an audience such as
his voice, were he an orator, could never cover—to the number, it
may be, of half-a-million.   Nor are the incentives of the political
partizan wanting in the journalist whose predilection is for art,
and who cares to advance the interests of this or that school of
painting ; or whose passion is literature or music, and who wishes
to mould the public taste on his own : or who, as a private friend,
desires to say a good word for the artist, the actor, or the author
whose personality he loves, and whose work merits the recognition.
These are pleasures keen enough to make life worth living, and
they are peculiar to the literary career.

And journalism has not only its own rewards; it is also "a
stepping-stone to higher things," and to more lucrative things.
Just as literature, apart from journalism, brought Bulwer a barony,
and Barry Cornwall and Forster profitable Lunacy Commissioner-

ships, and just as Mr. Edward Jenkins, in 1874, had no other introduction to the electors of Dundee than "Ginx's Baby," so also has journalism pure and simple its extraneous distinctions and rewards. In the present Parliament the profession is more numerously and strongly represented than it ever was before. Mr. Passmore Edwards, who is proprietor of the *Echo* and of a building journal, and to whom Mr. Gladstone recently wrote, "You have been surpassed by none in the courage and constancy with which you have contended through evil times for a just policy abroad," sits for Salisbury; while an ex-editor of the *Echo*, Mr. Arthur Arnold, a brother of Mr. Edwin Arnold of the *Daily Telegraph*, represents Salford. Newcastle-on-Tyne has given to Mr. Joseph Cowen, proprietor of the spiritedly conducted *Newcastle Chronicle*, a colleague in Mr. Ashton Dilke, proprietor of the *Weekly Dispatch*, and brother of Sir Charles Dilke, Chelsea's senior member, himself the owner of the *Athenæum*. Mr. Courtney, of *The Times*, retains his seat for Liskeard, and the proprietor of that paper is still the member for

Berks. Mr. Labouchere, part proprietor of the *Daily News* and editor of *Truth*, divides the representation of Northampton with Mr. Bradlaugh, who projected the *National Reformer.* South-East Lancashire sends to Parliament, in the person of Mr. William Agnew, not merely a magnate among picture dealers, but one of the proprietors of *Punch.* Mr. Beresford-Hope owns the *Saturday Review.* Mr. Macliver, who won at Plymouth, is the proprietor of the spirited *Western Daily Press.* Ireland sends a strong contingent, among whom are Mr. Edward Dwyer Gray, of the *Freeman's Journal;* Mr. A. M. Sullivan, late editor of the *Nation;* his brother, T. D. Sullivan, now the editor and proprietor of that paper, and Mr. Sexton, the latter's associate editor; Mr. T. P. O'Connor, author of the scathing *Life of Lord Beaconsfield;* Mr. F. H. O'Donnell, a hard-working journalist on the London press; Mr. Lysaght Finigan, Mr. Parnell's " lieutenant " — and Mr. Justin McCarthy, novelist, historian, and leader-writer on the *Daily*

News. Mr. Alfred Austin, indeed, whose name has long been rescued from the anonymity of leader-writing or book-reviewing in the *Standard* by achievements in the open literary world, tried for a seat and failed; so did Mr. Thomas Gibson Bowles, of *Vanity Fair;* so did Mr. John Morley, editor of the *Fortnightly* and the *Pall Mall Gazette;* and so did Sir Algernon Borthwick, of the *Morning Post,* who was consoled by a knighthood for his narrow electoral defeat. Some of these names—those belonging to the inheritors of wealthy newspaper proprietorships, for instance—do little to point our moral; but there are others among them which represent men who do distinctly owe to their connection with the journalistic world, and to it alone, their position in life and in the legislature.

Then, again, journalism has supported men while they kept terms and were called to the bar; witness, as one among many, the late Hepworth Dixon, who also obtained temporary but lucrative Exhibition Commissionerships, and was, moreover, invited to contest Marylebone in 1868. Once a barrister, the journalist may go on to higher things still, even till he shall occupy the woolsack itself, like Lord Chancellor Campbell, who walked from Scotland with the traditional trifle in his pocket to begin life as a reporter on the *Morning Chronicle.* The same paper gave the same employment to Dickens, who, like many others, passed from this more mechanical rank of journalism, not to the law, but to authorship—to a more sympathetic, human, and brilliant fame. Such emphatically was his who, young and utterly alone in the world, unhelped by word or act of man, serving letters alone and aided by them only, reached an unshared throne of renown in the memory and love of men. .

II. The Seamy Side.

AVING examined the fair side, we proceed to explore the seamy. And on turning up the other surface, one sees at a glance that what was on the first sight an ornament, shows through the stuff, and appears here with a reverse and a very ugly effect. In other words, the gain of the journalistic beginner in being able to dispense in part with an apprenticeship, and in requiring no heavy stock-in-trade before he begins, or tries to begin, business, has, from another point of view than that which we took in the last chapter, its serious disadvantages. For this very ease, and this partial exemption from the responsibilities and difficulties of other callings, inevitably give to literature somewhat of the character of a *pis-aller*. A boy is rarely brought up to a profession for which a bringing up does not seem a necessity; he rather turns to it in after years when he has failed elsewhere, through loss of fortune, through incapacity in the calling chosen for him, or because that calling has disappointed his hopes. And, besides being a *pis-aller* through its exemption from training,

literature is calculated to be an over-crowded profession through its exemption from the usual preliminary sacrifice of capital—two immunities which must always tend to keep down the profits of literary work. Moreover, they induce a large number of people to make literature a part-career, thus damaging it for those who have no other means of support. With far more justice than the tradesman could the journalist cry out against the Government Office men, whose contributions (and on official paper too!) pour into the editorial letter-boxes of London; but he does not do so; he frankly accepts the conditions of his calling, though he may momentarily regret, when he hears of men with large public or private incomes writing at a price which entails semi-starvation if entirely depended on for support, that there is not a little more trade unionism among authors. And yet, curiously enough, it is exactly these semi-professionals whom we have heard denouncing in the most unmeasured terms the miserable pittance to be earned on the press—a proceeding which always reminds us of the case of the man who, having murdered his father and mother, appealed to the court for mercy because he was an orphan.

Those who are mentally or physically incapable of hard work, will find a seamy side indeed to the journalistic career. Above all things it is laborious—not as practised in the *ad libitum* manner of the beginner, who may or may not, as he feels inclined, produce his day's task; but as followed by the professional

journalist, who has achieved, say, the somewhat eminent success
of a post on the staff of a fairly good daily paper. In that
position an amount of application which would bring name and
fame to the barrister, the clergyman or the doctor, only suffices
for the bare fulfilment of his duty. Say he is a special correspondent; his fate is as little in his own hands as is that of the
Jesuit priest whom we have been taught to commiserate, because
he is liable to be ordered by his general to change his address from
Mount Street, Berkeley Square, to India, or China, at a moment's
notice. The newspaper correspondent, without the stimulus of a
religious motive, but simply as part of the year's labour that
secures him what a successful barrister would hardly call a
decently good income, holds himself in daily readiness to start
for an exhibition in Sydney, or a royal wedding in Vienna, or a
funeral at Madrid; or he is told off to study Nihilism on the spot,
in a Russian mid-winter; or sent across a burning African desert
on perilous enterprise; nor is there ever a battle fought without his
presence, where English or European interests are involved. And
if the soldier and sailor in active service have a harder time than
the correspondent who accompanies them, it must not be forgotten
that he often shares their risks—a deadly climate, for instance,
is as fatal to him as to them—but gains none of their glory; that
they are facing perils in fulfilment of their career, and he only as
an accident of his; and that whereas they retire in middle life

with half-pay and pensions, and often with titular distinctions, it was never known, we suppose, that a newspaper correspondent was idle till he came to the long obscurity of the grave. A retired journalist, in the true sense of the word—that is to say, one who retired on the money made in a purely journalistic career—is an individual whose acquaintance we have yet to make.

Of course there are members of a newspaper staff who stay at home at ease. Not much ease either, in the case, for instance, of the political leader-writer, who turns night into day to work upon latest information. For instance, Mr. Justin McCarthy, before he was elected for Longford, was a diligent attender at the House of Commons, listening in the gallery for the last word of a Ministerial statement, or of an Opposition attack; and then, at perhaps one or two o'clock in the morning, sitting down to finish the leader which the readers of the *Daily News* conned over at breakfast, or in early trains. Or, let us take the case of the sub-editor, or co-editor, of another of the London dailies, whom we have in mind. He is so chained to his work that he is only able to give a dinner-party or to dine out once in the week (a limitation which would be a substantial grievance to a man of equal eminence in another profession); and on this solitary festive occasion he is often obliged to leave his guests or his hosts to write a leader on some unexpected event. He has only one morning—that of Saturday—in which he can take the solace of gun or line, or mere country

air; not only must he be up late at night, but he is impatient
to rise early in the morning, so that he may con the "latest
intelligence" of the rival dailies, to satisfy himself that they have
not outdone his own; his brain is not only active with constant
production, but worn with responsibility; and his annual holiday,
especially if the political times are stirring, is none too long.

Nor does the hard labour of the sub-editor, the special
correspondent, or the leader-writer abate one jot if the pinnacle of
the profession—a head editorship—be attained. Let us see how
it fared with him who sat on the throne of journalism, the late Mr.
Delane. "He had," says one of his
friends, "the instincts of family
affection almost to excess;" yet
for many years he could only run
down on Saturday to bury himself for a few hours in his Berkshire
home, domestic life in town being obviously out of the question for
one who for nearly half of each year saw the sun rise every morning,
not after what it would be a mockery to call his night's rest, but
before it. He was a warm friend, yet how few were the hours he
could devote to friendship! His love of company was something
more than the natural and universal preference shown by educated
men for what is called good society, and his personal qualities
made him welcome wherever he went; nevertheless, when he joined
a friendly circle at dinner, as soon as the clock struck ten he

disappeared. "Few," says the friend already referred to, "can estimate what it was for Mr. Delane to withdraw as unobservedly and as early as he could from the assembled guests, before they had joined the ladies, to spend many hours selecting materials, pruning redundant paragraphs, fining down tedious narratives, deciphering manuscripts, correcting proofs, harmonizing discordant intelligence, discovering the sense of telegraphic riddles, and often finishing by sacrificing the editorial labour of many hours to make room for some bulky and important, but very late, arrival, that must be published, at whatever cost." And this gives us a glimpse of the huge and constant responsibility of such a post—a responsibility which must needs have its own inevitable effect upon health. Of course there is only one Delane, but there are a hundred other editors of whom the same tale may be told in their degree. Of this burden on journalistic eminence, however, we shall say no more here, as the subject comes within the scope of the chapter headed " In an Editor's Chair."

Laborious, scantily paid, the profession is moreover inglorious, for all but the very few, unless, indeed, we accept that impersonal glory—the consciousness of good work done and effective power wielded anonymously—as the satisfaction of the natural ambition. Many a journalist spends himself—the best of his intellect and the flower of his days—in speaking to a public which is and will always be utterly ignorant of his individuality. Nor is his anonymity merely that of a writer who chooses to mask his person under one *nom de plume* but whose work is appreciated as the utterance of some one man; it is his fate to bury himself under a far profounder incognito than this—nay, he breaks up his individuality into a thousand separate fragments, not one of which bears the stamp of his name. The man is scattered and lost, the character of his work is dissipated by dissemination, and nothing remains but the influence of that work falling as it may when sown broadcast; though, by an apt compensation, the impersonality adds so much to this influence that few who are journalists at heart are found to lament it. A newspaper on the Continent, for instance, with its acknowledged articles, has never had and can never have the weight in public opinion which an English newspaper possesses. The unrivalled position of the English press is due fully as much to its anonymity as to its freedom. But this train of thought brings us back again to the fairer side of the literary career; and that is the side which we would leave uppermost after all.

IN AN EDITOR'S CHAIR.

N editor is a much-abused man. Con-
tributors who think he has neglected them,
or failed to appreciate them, or "cut out"
or "written in" where he should not, do
not spare him; the readers of his paper
do not measure terms when any single
thing in his many columns strikes them as
false in taste or below the mark in intelligence. Above all is a
slip from classical English proclaimed aloud with a kind of gay
triumph among amateurs who have infinite leisure for the criticism
of articles hastily revised, perhaps at dead of night, and after long
hours of labour. Cobbett made the columns of *The Times* his
happy hunting-grounds for grammatical mistakes, and his example
has been followed with less point often since then. This is a very
cheap sort of censure, and only shows how little the critic has
reflected on the duties and difficulties of an editor's position.
Nor are these sufficiently taken to heart by the amateur authors
already alluded to — even though many among them have no
greater ambition in life than to sit in an editor's chair. In their

imagination it is the throne of an easy power which may sway opinion and legislate on politics, ethics, and the arts. They have formed no idea to themselves as to the realities of work and responsibility—realities hardly to be matched in any other position of modern life. Of the editor's labour we have already spoken labour of the pen at actual composition and at endless letter-writing; labour of the judgment at selection and decision; labour of the eyes at proof-reading; labour of the tongue and temper in dealing with men whom for various reasons it is necessary to see —from the Minister of State, on whose leisure he must attend, to the veriest bore who is too useful a person or too good-natured a goose to affront; labour of the journalistic instinct in putting forward what will "take," and of the intelligence at rapid sifting of conflicting evidence;—and all this in the hurry of going to press and the anxiety to obtain the latest news, which, by arriving in unexpected quantity, or failing to come at all, may throw out all calculations at the last moment. But great as is the strain of this hard work, it is light compared with the burden of responsibility which otherwise attaches to his post. And it is this responsibility, rather than the mere manual and mental labour, that we are about to consider.

"When I remember," said Lord Beaconsfield at the Edinburgh Corn Exchange in 1867, "the interests of these British Isles, so vast, so various and so complicated—when I even recall the differences of race, which, however blended, leave a very significant characteristic—when I recollect that the great majority of the population of the United Kingdom rise every day and depend for their daily sustenance on their daily labour—when I recollect the delicate nature of our credit, more wonderful in my opinion than all our accumulated capital—when I remember that it is on the common sense, the prudence, and the courage of a community thus circumstanced that depends the fate of uncounted millions in ancient provinces, and that around the globe there is a circle of domestic settlements that watch us for example and inspiration —when I know that not a sun rises on a British Minister that does not bring him care and even inexpressible anxiety—an unexpected war, a disturbed and discontented colony, a pestilence, a famine, a mutiny, a declining trade, a decaying revenue, a collapse of credit, perhaps some insane and fantastic conspiracy—I declare I very often wonder where there is the strength of heart to deal with such colossal circumstances." We shall hardly be exaggerating if we draw a parallel between the anxieties of the British Minister, thus graphically portrayed, and those of the British editor of a leading daily paper, or in their lesser measure of those of the editors of important weekly papers which deal with current events and criticise public affairs. Take the case of the editor of *The Times*, as an extreme but still a representative one. He presides over his staff as a Premier over his Cabinet,

and on his choice of a policy—a choice he is sometimes called
upon to make in a hurry—the fate of his paper, involving a capital
of hundreds of thousands, in some cases of more than a million,
depends. It is a mistake to suppose that a powerful organ can
always carry its readers with it; on the contrary, they are
easily alienated. And on an important and perhaps involved
national question, to see the right line, to take it, and never to
falter in pursuing it, is a task as difficult and delicate as that of
any public man in any capacity whatever. Differences of nation
and creed concern an editor perhaps even more than they concern a Minister of State. Then an article in *The Times* produces
fluctuations in the money market—the paper itself fluctuating
with those fluctuations—and even affects the national credit.
Nay, upon its tone towards foreign powers often depends the
tremendous alternative of peace or war. To be right and correct
and in accord with enlightened public opinion in far smaller things
than these—in the merest details of the merest trivialities—is an
essential effort on the part of an editor; the slightest slip may
by some accidental circumstance assume large proportions,
and in a moment his credit be gone. The consciousness of this
is a weight incommensurately greater than that which is experienced
in other professions—by the barrister under his crucial brief, by
the doctor under his most critical case. The one may lose a
single client, and the other fail over a single patient, but the world

will not blame either, if he has taken proper pains: while the failure of an editor is apparent to the whole of his huge constituency, and the chances are that no one will inquire into its cause, or care whether he blundered conscientiously or not.

All this was so feelingly put forth in the memoir of Mr. Delane which appeared in *The Times*, and was, as we know, so feelingly read by those who on other papers bore a like or an only lighter burden, that we cannot do better than reproduce its salient passages here : —" An editor, it has often been said, sometimes not very seriously, must know everything. He must, at least, never be found at fault, and must be always equal to the occasion as to the personal characteristics, the concerns, the acts and utterances of those who are charged with the government of this great Empire. But this is only one of many points, some even more difficult, because more special and more apt to lie for a time out of the scope of ordinary vigilance. Since the year 1841 the world has seen unprecedented improvements in naval and military material and tactics, not slowly making their way as curiosities that might take their time, but forced into notice by frequent reminders of their necessity. Europe has seen not only two or three but many revolutions, wars unexampled for their dimensions, their cost and their results ; many dynasties overthrown, an Empire rise and fall, another all but finally dismembered amid a scramble over the spoil, and several re-unifications effected beyond even the hopes

of former times. Scientific discovery in every department of
knowledge has been more than ever active, and that in the practical
bearings which claim the notice of the public from day to day.
Never before have the earth and the sea so freely revealed their
resources and their treasures.   Continents supposed to be
protected from intrusive curiosity by intolerable heat, by untam-
able savagery, or by national jealousy, have been traversed in all'
directions by explorers whose volumes have been as familiar as
our Continental handbooks. Within this period have been the
gold discoveries and the new communities founded on them. It
is commonly said that the English never really learn geography or
history till" [these are] "forced upon their acquaintance by wars or
other disasters. This shows how much has to be learnt if any one
has to keep pace with the times. The American Civil War, our
own Indian Mutiny, and the occupation of France by the German
armies, are events which the future student of history may find
comprised in a few paragraphs, but the record and explanation
of them day by day for many months involved particulars sufficient
to fill many bulky volumes. With a large class of critics, a small
mistake counts as much as a large one, but everybody is liable to
make mistakes, and an editor labours under the additional danger
of too readily accepting the words of writers, some of whom will
always be too full of their ideas to pay needful attention to such
matters. These are days of Blue-books, of enormous correspon-

dence, of tabular returns, of statistics twisted into every possible form, of averages and differences always on supposition to be carefully remembered, of numerical comparisons everybody challenges if they are not in his own favour, and of statements that if they possess the least novelty or other interest are sure to be picked to pieces. It frequently happens that a long night's work has to be thrown away, including many carefully-revised columns of printed matter, to make room for an overgrown Parliamentary debate, a budget of important despatches, or a speech made in the provinces. Often has it been said at two in the morning that a very good paper has been printed and destroyed to make way for a paper that very few will read—none, perhaps, except a few Parliamentary gentlemen looking out for passages which, if they don't read well, must have been incorrectly reported. As an instance of what may happen to an editor, the Quarterly Return of the Revenue once came with an enormous error, an addition instead of subtraction, or *vice versâ*. The writer who had to comment on it jotted down the principal figures, and the totals, which were unexpected, and returned the original for the printers. It was not till an hour after midnight that, on a sight of the Return in print, the error was perceived, and corrected, without a word of remark, by the paper. Of course, the comments had to be re-written and carefully secured from error. . . . The work of an editor can only be appreciated by those who have had the fortune to have some little experience of it. The editor of a London daily newspaper is held answerable for every word in 48, and sometimes 60, columns. The merest slip of the pen, an epithet too much, a wrong date, a name misspelt, or with a wrong initial before it, a mistake as to some obscure personage only too glad to seize the opportunity of showing himself, the misinterpretation of some passage perhaps incapable of interpretation, the most trifling offence to the personal or national susceptibility of those who do not even profess to care for the feelings of others, may prove not only disagreeable but even costly mistakes: but they are among the least to which an editor is liable. As it is impossible to say what a night may bring forth, and the most important intelligence is apt to be the latest, it will often find him with none to share his responsibility, his colleagues being either pre-engaged on other matters or no longer at hand. The editor must be on the spot till the paper is sent to the press, and make decisions on which not only the approval of the British public, but great events, and even great causes, may hang. All the more serious part of his duties has to be discharged at the end of a long day's work, a day of interruptions and conversations, of letter-reading and letter-writing, when mind and body are not what they were twelve hours ago, and wearied nature is putting in her gentle pleas. An editor cannot husband his strength for the night's battle by comparative repose in the solitude of a study or the freshness of green fields.

He must see the world, converse with its foremost or busiest actors, be open to information, and on guard against error. All this ought to be borne in mind by those who complain that journalism is not infallibly accurate, just, and agreeable. Their complaints are like those of the Court lord who found fault with the disagreeable necessities of warfare." How much indeed has happened since the days when Cowper wrote of

> "The folio of four pages, happy work,
> Which not e'en critics criticise."

And even this is not a complete picture of an editor's toils and sufferings. Just as it is necessary for a paper to stand well with the general public, so is it important for its editor to stand well with his own intimate public—his private friends and the writers on his staff. How to reconcile their claims on his kindness and consideration with his duty to the world is often a difficult problem. His outside friends may be politicians or writers on whom his columns are bound to pass an unfavourable verdict; while from a host of acquaintances, of both sexes, he receives daily, and is generally obliged to deny, the solicitations incessantly made to all who have anything to do with public opinion. And what tact is needed in such cases to give a denial, yet not to give offence! Nor is it less difficult or less requisite for the editor to be on friendly working relations with his staff. Each one of these has a personality of his own, an experience to which deference is due, and at the same time a political or a religious bias, which a wide acquaintance with the *personnel* of the movements of the day only serves to emphasize.   Yet often the editor must hurriedly set his assistant's deliberate judgment aside ; and must always eliminate the merely personal feeling, and put public feeling in its stead, knowing, as has been well said, that, "great as is the audacity of inner consciousness in these days, its place is not in an editor's room."   And this (though it seems paradoxical to say so) as regards the editor himself as much as any member of his staff.   For the good editor is the man who has the fewest hobbies, or having them, rides them least, and who is able to raise himself above the level of party passion and personal inclination, to direct the course of his journal as from a judge's bench for impartiality, as from a true statesman's standpoint for prescience and long-sighted precision.   And as he is and ought to be impersonal in what he says, so he is and ought to be impersonal in his very way of saying it.   Thus the editorial "we" is not only a more modest yet more dignified but also a more absolutely accurate pronoun than "I" for the leader-writer's use. This is still more obviously the fact when, as often happens, the writer, or the editor who inspires the writer, takes his cue not only from what his trained perception tells him is most right and politic (*pace* any little personal weaknesses of his own), but from actual consultation with his wisest colleagues, with the heads of his Parliamentary party, and with all the best authorities at command. His " leader " is thus the pronouncement of the collective wisdom of a board of direction, and cannot without the absurdest confusion be classed with the opinion uttered at random by a man over his matutinal coffee or at his club—an opinion which he may change to-morrow, while that of a newspaper must never be recorded except after such deliberation as will allow it to be consistently maintained.

· When the *Morning Chronicle* was bought by Mr. Gladstone, the Duke of Newcastle, and Lord Herbert of Lea, to be placed in the hands of Mr. Cook (afterwards editor of the *Saturday Review*), and conducted from the unpopular platform of Puseyism in religion as well as Peelism in politics, not all their combined influence, ability, and capital, could prevent a decrease in circulation and an actual average loss of from £10,000 to £12,000 a year. In 1854— according to Mr. Grant, a not infallible authority—they sold the paper to Serjeant Glover, agreeing to give him £3,000 annually for three years on condition that he should continue to advocate the same principles—an arrangement, if really made, curiously at variance with certain floating impressions as to supposed editorial freedom from the restraining influences of capital ; and the Serjeant accepted a further subsidy from France to support the Napoleonic Idea. But the public would have none of it ; and the journal, whose "we" had been accepted during ninety years of broad and spirited management, was hurled into bankruptcy by becoming the organ of a clique. Used in a class journal, of course the "we" represents only a class, and is nevertheless legitimate—always supposing the journal does not pretend to be more than it is. But the great dailies and weeklies are much more than this, and must represent the thought of a multitude, not the whim of a unit; and let us add our conviction that no editor or proprietor of such would ever pander to a popular feeling which he knew to be injurious to the welfare of the State. All this is what even a thoughtful writer like Emerson may fail to comprehend. "Was ever," he exclaims, "such arrogancy as the tone of *The Times* ? Every slip of an Oxonian or Cambridgian, who writes his first leader, assumes 'we' subdued the earth before 'we' sat down to write this particular *Times*. One would think the world was on its knees to *The Times* office for its daily breakfast. But the arrogance is calculated. Who would care for it if it 'surmised,' or 'dared to confess,' or 'ventured to predict'? No; *it is so*, and so it shall be." The idea of a "slip" of an undergraduate trying his 'prentice pen in the most important department of our most important paper—that of *The Times* leading articles—is sufficiently grotesque, and shows how very far the most intelligent alien is from understanding the seriousness and the solidity of our great national organs.

All journalists, therefore, and everyone who has the best

interests of journalism at heart, ought, we would earnestly urge, to deprecate any public attempt to associate a newspaper with its *personnel* in the sense of attacking writers by name for the anonymous opinions which their newspaper expresses; or of attacking a newspaper for the private shortcomings, real or supposed, of any individual member of its proprietary or staff. This kind of banter, which has become so much the fashion of late, may raise a momentary smile, but it must in the end be fatal to the liberty and prestige of the press, while it indefinitely increases that ·burden which already weighs too heavily on an editor, for whom, be it understood, we are claiming no licence to be untruthful, but only leave to be, in the exercise of duty, as impersonal as the barrister, the clergyman, the statesman, the monarch, the pontiff, and the judge.

From all this it must be apparent that the qualifications of an editor are not only or chiefly of a literary order. He must be before all things a man of the world, conversant with many subjects, and able to get on well with his fellows, some of whom are also men of the world, and some of whom are not. Mr. Delane, for instance, never wrote in *The Times,* but he directed the policy of those who did, even down to the minutest particular, a habit which the following note very characteristically illustrates :—" My dear sir,—You may review——, if you like, a most admirable book; but before you do this please to write me a memoir, rather eulogistic than otherwise, but ao4 puffing, of Sir William Mansfield, who, after resigning the chief command in India, has just been appointed to the chief command in Ireland.—Ever faithfully yours, M. T. DELANE." Among weekly journals the *Saturday Review* has been issued for years together without an article from the editor's pen.

Although what we have hitherto said about the troubles of editing, and the kind of capacity requisite to cope with them, applies principally to the daily and a portion of the weekly press, it holds good also of all editing, in a greater or a less degree. Even a monthly will not be successfully conducted by a *littérateur*, however brilliant, unless with his literary ability he combines a faculty for business, a power to endure drudgery, and a variety of personal qualities not often met with in any one man. Coleridge, curiously enough, succeeded, as editor of the *Morning Post*, in greatly increasing its circulation ; but, as a rule, editors are made of sterner stuff. "I can find any number of men of genius to write for me, but very seldom one of common sense," an editor of *The Times* remarked to Moore. Without endorsing this saying in its hard, excessive *brusquerie*, we accept in a modified manner the truth it contains, and recommend it to the careful attention of amateurs, who must after all perceive that it is not easy to sit in that editorial chair which Campbell, Moore, Leigh Hunt, Carlyle, Lytton, Thackeray, Charles Dickens, George Sala, and Anthony Trollope were forced by one cause or another to abandon.

A MISCELLANEOUS CHAPTER.

E have somewhat strayed from the amateur, to whom our first chapters were addressed, in the excursion we have made to the fields of professional life. Our excuse is that no amateur who is capable of taking regular rank will be content to remain an amateur— a fact which distinguishes literature from the other arts. A reluctance to sell a picture, to lecture, act, sing, or play for money is common enough in certain classes—or if such reluctance is wearing away, a little shyness lingers when the market-matters of sale and purchase are in question. But no one ever has been, or ever will be, in any degree ashamed of pocketing a cheque for literary work, and the most hypersensitive have no fear of losing caste by selling the pure production of their brains. This is probably because no personal appearance or performance for money is involved, and also that no *material* is the subject of barter. Mr. Trollope may choose to call literature a trade ; nevertheless the *littérateur* is in no sense a tradesman. Besides all this, letters

are and will always remain altogether the noblest of the arts—the one art, perhaps, with which society could not by any possibility dispense—our very thinking in daily life having taken literary form, and some kind of reading being really as necessary to us as bread ; whereas a civilization deprived of music, painting, or the drama, is at least conceivable. No literary amateur, then, puts any limit before himself. He aims at a professional standing even when he does not intend literature to be his only profession ; and consequently there is not in this art the line of demarcation between the artist and the dilettante which exists in the others ; nor have we separated them in our survey.

By no means exhaustive has been this review of one of the most distinctive developments of the modern world. There are joys and sorrows, for instance, in the literary career, on which we have not touched. Of the former, one of the keenest is the sensation produced on the novice by his first success. Merely to see himself in print for the first time is a pleasure almost overwhelming, if only for the "promise that it closes." If that great event could fall flat, it would assuredly be a sign that his heart was not in his work ; that his work, consequently, was not worthy of him ; and that it behoved him to seek forthwith for some occupation which either *would* have power over his emotions, or in which emotion would be altogether out of place. A success in tea, or in banking, or in conveyancing, will always leave him master of himself; but he should let the arts alone, if he considers unbroken self-possession as a necessary part of his dignity. Charles Dickens, as we have already seen, does not hesitate to confess the happy tears with which he saw his first published words, and the nearer our beginner's experience comes to his, so much the more hope will there be that the career of the one may in some degree resemble that of the other. Out of the abundance of the heart the mouth speaketh, we are told; and if the young writer have sent out words from the real abundance of his heart, he has merited the delight of seeing them winged for flight into the corners of the world. Nor will any art or any pursuit yield him a more just enjoyment, or a more lasting one; it will not wear out at the fifth repetition, nor at the fiftieth, so long as his work is honest work; his satisfaction will be calmer, indeed, but as solid as ever.

We come to one of the sorrows of the career when we deplore that this moving, touching, thrilling moment of a first publication should so often be marred by a little matter which is enough to turn a triumph into a mortification. Everyone who has passed through the experience will know that we refer to the sore subject of misprints. The beginner is more liable than another to this form of disappointment and annoyance, because he generally sends in his tentative MS. to some comparatively obscure periodical, the printing department of which is not a model of

efficiency; or because an editor may not think a casual contribution worth the trouble of a despatch of proofs. Amateur authors
are largely to be blamed for the frequent neglect of this precaution and courtesy on the part of an editor; if they would
more generally take the trouble to complete their work, finally
and irrevocably, before sending it in—if, that is, they could be
trusted to correct in proof the compositor's errors merely, and
not to re-write and polish up their own sentences (which they
should have done in the MS.), they would often have the security
and satisfaction of receiving the coveted slips. Such afterthoughts
of an author entail on an editor serious expense, which he cannot
be blamed for avoiding. Yet it must be owned that misprints are
intolerable. The absurdity of the errors—and they hardly ever
fail of a poignant absurdity—the utter impotence of the unhappy
writer, who has no means whatever of retrieving his character for
common sense, or even sanity, are calculated to drive him to
temporary despair. Feelingly does an anonymous (we believe a
Transatlantic) bard sing the sorrows which embitter what would
otherwise be a moment of entire glory :—

ON SEEING MY FIRST POEM IN A NEWSPAPER.

Ah ! here it is ! I'm famous now—
  An author and a poet !
It really is in print—ye gods,
  How proud I'll be to show it !

And gentle Anna—what a thrill
  Will animate her breast
To read these ardent lines, and know
  To whom they are addressed.

Why, bless my soul—here's something
  strange !
What can the paper mean
By talking of the "graceful brooks
That gander o'er the green ? "
And here's a T instead of R,
  Which makes it "tippling rill ; "
"We'll seek the shad," instead of shade,
  And "hell," instead of hill.

"They look so"—what ?—I recollect
'Twas "sweet," and then 'twas "kind."
And now to think the stupid fool
  For bland has printed "blind."
Was ever such provoking work ?—
  'Tis curious, by the bye,
How anything is rendered blind
  By giving it an eye.

"Hast thou no tears ?"—the T's left
  out ;
  "Hast thou no ears ? " instead.
"I hope that thou art dear " is put
  "I hope that thou art dead."
Whoever saw in such a space
  So many blunders crammed ?
"Those gentle eyes bedimmed " is spelt,
  "Those gentle eyes bedammed."

"Thou art the same " is rendered
  "lame,"
It really is too bad ;
And here, because an I is out,
  My "lovely maid " is "mad."
"Where are the muses fed, that thou
  Shouldst live so long unsung ? "
Thus read my version : here it is,
  "Shouldst live so long unhung."

I'll read no more. What shall I do?
  I'll never dare to send it.
The paper 's scattered far and wide—
  'Tis now too late to mend it.
Oh, Fame ! thou cheat of human bliss !
  Why did I ever write ?
I wish my poem had been burnt
  Before it saw the light.

I wish I had that editor,
  About a half-a-minute,
I'd *bang* him to my heart's content,
  And with an H begin it.
I'd *jam* his body, eyes, and nose,
  And spell it with a D ;
And send him to that *kill* of his—
  He spells it with an E.

Nor is it the amateur alone who is familiar with this dismay.
All through life the literary man is liable—often owing to a sloven-
liness of handwriting—to be misprinted; and he will never like it,
nor perhaps ever bear it with equanimity. He will find, too,
that when he is misprinted it is generally in the very passages on
which his affections were principally set, and his sensations, if

milder than those of the *débutant*, are far from pleasant. In all
cases the mortification—more keen according to the inexperience
of the victim—is sufficient to neutralize the pleasure—also more
keen according to the freshness of the author—of an appearance
in print.

With these and many other joys and sorrows are responsibilities
to which we have little space to allude, but which bear a larger
part in literary life than in perhaps any other career, not even
excepting religion, medicine and statesmanship.   And of the
two branches of literature—authorship and journalism—the latter
is assuredly the most heavily burdened.   In one way only can the
anonymous wielder of public power become worthy of his influence,
and that is by letting conscience guide all the course of his professional life.   Mere prudence will not avail to fit him for his post,
which is, indeed, usually one of so great security, that prudence
would be of itself a quite insufficient motive for honourable
conduct.   The priest must answer to visible powers, to his bishop
and his people; the physician to his patient; the statesman to the
nation; but the anonymous journalist very frequently is responsible
only to himself, and so much the more seriously will he feel the
force of obligations for the breach of which he may never have to
suffer; so much the more fine will become the sensitiveness of
his self-respect, so much the more active his sympathies.   And
while drawing this picture—ideal, perhaps, but happily also quite

real—we need not necessarily be included among those who declaim against personal journalism, so long as personality is inoffensive to any private feeling. Subject to that condition, it is legitimate enough, and all the more legitimate as it is inevitable. It is no new thing. A writer in a "Society" paper recently retorted to the stock charge of personality, that the daily Court Circular chronicles are far more intimately and intrusively personal than the information collected under the gossiping headings of the weeklies: for custom alone causes us to accept the announcement that her Majesty walked on the slopes, and that one maid of honour was succeeded by another, as a matter of any concern whatever to the general public. The censors of personal journalism generally assume that the persons or personages who are the subject of it are aggrieved by their own prominent appearance in print; the journalist, however, knows that there is no such grievance felt, provided the gossip published is pleasant gossip—and no other kind should be allowed to appear. Another facile criticism consists in the charge of Americanism. We would, however, recommend a comparison between the chattiest of the decent London journals of this kind and their Transatlantic contemporaries. A glance will show that the difference is immeasurable; that there is a twang about the American personalities which high-class English journalism of the kind has never caught. Apart from this, the press of the great

Republic has much that our own may imitate with advantage, and which is so imitated by some of the most successful of the English papers. The brightly-written, readable, and non-political foreign correspondence which has sometimes appeared in the *Daily Telegraph* is an example of this. Let us remember that we are not altogether perfect, and that if the French press seems to us frivolous and the American flippant, ours is considered quite intolerably prosaic and heavy in Paris and New York. To amuse is an important function of the modern newspaper, and one which we hope will never be neglected; for we believe there is hardly a single editor—we cannot tax our memory with one—in England who would consciously allow his paper to be made the vehicle of private spite, though he might possibly be made the tool of a malicious contributor through ignorance or through one of those errors of judgment from which nobody is exempt, but which are visited more heavily on an editor than on anyone else. For the journalist's freedom from what is generally understood by responsibility does not by any means belong to an editor—whose broad shoulders, indeed, are made to bear the burdens of his whole staff.

It remains for those who are about to enter the profession to keep it as honourable and high-toned as it now is. If, from choice or necessity, they tread the quicksands of personal journalism, they must remember how Charles Dickens boiled over with indignation at what he considered to be an unwarranted attack on a private reputation. "When I think," he writes to Macready, "that every dirty speck upon the fair face of the Almighty's creation who writes in a filthy, beastly newspaper; every rotten-hearted panderer who has been beaten, kicked, and rolled in the kennel, yet struts it in the editorial 'We' once a week; every vagabond that an honest man's gorge must rise at; every living emetic in that noxious drug-shop, the press, can have his fling at such men and call them knaves and fools and thieves—I grow so vicious that with bearing hard upon my pen I break the nib down, and with keeping my teeth set make my jaws ache." These words—written in a moment· of characteristic excitement and irritation, may hardly be a necessary warning to any of the beginners whom we address; yet the temptation to "smart" scribbling is great; and all who are liable to it should remember that personalities which would not be spoken out at a club are not to be printed in a newspaper. Nor do we grudge the great novelist his exaggeration in straining for effect, if that effect is produced on the minds of those in whose hands is the future of journalism for evil or good. Let them have always before them the words of another great and sensitive man. "Ah! ye knights of the pen," exclaims Thackeray in the "Roundabout Papers," "may honour be your shield, and truth tip your lances! Be gentle to all gentle people. Be modest to women. Be tender to children. And as for the ogre humbug, out sword, and have at him."

Enough has been said in these pages to the new writer, That which is in want of encouragement—and it is a truism that merit is generally modest—will, we hope, find nothing to chill or dismay it in the frankest sincerity of what we have said; nor that which requires suppressing, to give it false hopes. What we have written has been designed—we do not disguise it—for hindrance of some, as well as for help of others. For we have aimed at writing the truth only; and the truth has this property, among many, that everyone will find in it what he most needs and can best assimilate.

LITERARY COPYRIGHT.

 FEW words may here be said on the subject of literary copyright, particularly in connection with the periodical press. The amateur who, compelled by some circumstance or other, regretfully publishes in a magazine a composition out of which he believes a fortune might be made under happier auspices, may be glad to be assured that he does not lose all right over his work because it has been used by an editor, unless there is a special agreement to that effect.

By 5 and 6 Victoria, Cap. 45, it is provided (*inter alia*) :—

(1). That the copyright in every article in an encyclopedia, review, or other periodical, shall belong to the proprietor of that periodical for the same term (*i.e.* forty years) as is allowed by the act to authors of books, whenever such article shall be contributed on the terms that the copyright therein shall belong to such proprietor and be paid for by him. On that point it has been settled that the proprietor acquires no copyright till payment has actually been made.

(2). After the term of twenty-eight years from the first publication of any article, the right of publishing the same in a separate form shall revert to the author for the remainder of the term (of forty years) given by the act ; and during such term of twenty-eight years the proprietor shall not publish any such article separately without previously obtaining the author's consent.

(3). Any author may reserve to himself the right to publish any such composition in a separate form, and he will then be entitled to the sole copyright in the separate publication.

Apart from the strict legal regulations on this matter, there is probably a recognised custom in the profession by which the copyright in articles is considered to belong to the writer, in the absence of any express contrary stipulation, such as that, for instance, which Messrs. Cassell, Petter, Galpin and Co. include in the printed receipt form sent out with all their payments for literary matter. It will be seen, however, that by the provisions of the Act above quoted, in all ordinary cases, even where he is the owner of the copyright, an editor cannot publish a contribution in a separate shape without the writer's consent, which may be withheld until it is worth his while to grant it. For example, in the case of *Mayhew* v. *Maxwell* the defendant was restrained from publishing in a separate form, without the plaintiff's permission, an article written by the plaintiff in a magazine called *The Welcome Guest.*

Between author and publisher in regard to a volume, the arrangement as to copyright is more simple than that between author and editor. The composition simply changes hands. Yet even in selling out-and-out to a bookseller the copyright of a MS., its author may feel well assured that if its publication should prove a great and an unexpected pecuniary success, he will share in those profits, even though he has no legal claim to do so. Fifty instances of the kind could be brought up to show that publishers are not devoid of moral justness on such occasions.

Mr. Carlyle once said to Charles Sumner, that "the strangest thing in the history of literature was his recent receipt of £50 from America, on account of his 'French Revolution,' which had never yielded him a farthing in Europe, and probably never would." And, indeed, the new world furnishes a grand audience for all worthy and memorable English utterances. The Americans are eminently a reading people ; literature is cultivated among solitary New England farms in a manner that is foreign to the customs of Old England ; almost every village in the Northern States has its free public library and reading-room ; and some English books which are little read at home are household words among the pastures of New Hampshire and Massachusetts. In fame and sympathy, then, America almost overpays our authors, but commercially the matter is notoriously otherwise, the absence of any satisfactory regulation as to international copyright leaving the remuneration of writers here, whose works are republished there, entirely to the chance benevolence of the American bookseller, who, naturally enough, does not care to pay much for a copyright

which he cannot legally protect. Into the intricate English law of
libel we do not propose to enter here. Suffice it to say that in any
difficulty of the kind, or in any question of copyright, authors will
find in Mr. George Lewis an adviser whose care, courtesy, and
consideration are only equalled by his ability and the legal experience he is known to have acquired in all matters relating to
authorship and the press.

TEN COMMANDMENTS: WITH REASONS AND REMARKS.

OPY" (the technical name of MSS. sent to the press) *must be written on only one side of the paper.* This because the sheets are often divided among a body of printers to secure expedition or to keep all hands employed. Of course it is especially on a daily that copy is set into type in a hurry. If, for instance, the last speech of a Parliamentary debate arrive an hour before the paper goes to press, the sheets are cut crossways into shreds or "takes," so that simultaneous printing produces the whole in a few minutes. The rule, however, applies to all MSS., whether sent to a daily paper or a quarterly review.

2. *Write on sheets of paper which are neither small enough to be scrappy nor large enough to be cumbrous on the printer's case.* No exact size can be mentioned as universally preferred by compositors; but the most convenient of all is perhaps foolscap quarto, which measures about seven inches by eight. A small post-octavo

(about four inches by seven) and a large post-octavo (five inches by eight) are also popular sizes.

3. *Leave plenty of space in margins and between lines* for your own and editorial corrections. Then a whole page of MS. need not be recopied because a sentence is altered. Every line may have a correction if legibly made.

4. *Use white paper rather than blue ;* because the writing stands out more distinctly—an important consideration with the compositor, who often works by gaslight.

5. *Use ink, and black ink* — for the same reason. ˙Pencil-writing is fainter and generally smudges ; moreover it catches the light at certain angles, and becomes invisible to the printer, whose head, unless he stoops, is a couple of feet distant from his "copy."

6. *Write plainly.* Distinct penmanship is an immense desideratum with both, editor and printer. Excellent contributions have gone into the waste-paper basket because editors, always busy, have not time or patience to decipher hieroglyphics. It is true that not all established journalists write very readably—as some of the autographs scattered through these pages sufficiently show. In fact, much rapid writing, as Lord Lytton somewhere says, destroys even a beautiful hand. But in the case of a professional, on the staff of a paper, his contributions are frequently never read by the editor until they are in type, and the burden of the bad

writing falls on the compositor alone; the amateur, however, will certainly feel the disadvantage of writing an illegible hand. Above all, write proper names and technical phrases in characters as clear as print. A compositor deciphers cleverly and almost instinctively where the words are those in ordinary use; but where they are out of the common run, of course he can only guess at them, and goes proverbially wide of the mark.

7. *Number your pages of MS.*

' 8. *Write your name and address in a corner of the first page*, where it is sure to be seen, instead of on the back of a sheet, or in an accompanying letter where it is more likely than not to be overlooked or lost.

9. *Be punctual.* A remembrance of this trite admonition will often stand a journalist in good stead. A man of mediocre talent who always sends his copy in at the right time is worth more to an editor than a genius who cannot be depended on. A few hints about sending-in days may not be amiss. Weeklies generally require latest copy at least two days before they are published, and almost without exception they are published a day or two earlier than the date they bear. Saturday's *Punch* is a Wednesday institution; Wednesday's *World* is read on Tuesday afternoon; just as the evening papers are on the railway stalls when we oversleep a little in the morning. The *World*, for example, goes to press on Monday night to be ready for actual publication on Tuesday

afternoon, and though down to Monday night it is possible to insert anything of special importance the standing rule is that copy shall reach the editor on Saturday morning, or failing that, be posted by members of the staff straight to the printer not later than Sunday night. Again, the *Graphic* goes to press in two parts —that which contains the story and standing matter earlier in the week than that which is devoted to current comment and to news. Obviously, a contribution loses half its chance of insertion when probably more than enough copy to fill the whole paper has been already sent in. Even some of the monthly magazines, less concerned than the weeklies with passing affairs, are prepared for the press a fortnight or more before they are published. Contributions, for instance, to one of Messrs. Cassell, Petter, and Galpin's monthlies for April will sometimes be asked for by even the first of February; and the principal contents of *Good Words* are arranged nearly a year in advance. Stories for Christmas numbers are ordered in the height of summer; and verses apostrophizing snow are composed with the thermometer at 80 deg.; just as Hogarth's poet indited an ode to riches while his wife was dunned for the milk-score. This will account to the beginner for many vexatious editorial delays and refusals, and will impress on him the necessity of taking time by the forelock when sending his contributions to the press.

2. *Mark the "proofs" of any accepted contribution sent for*

correction according to the technical system, which avoids endless confusion, and which every compositor understands. The publishers have added an advertisement sheet at the end of this book which sets forth this professional method of correcting for the press.

A DICTIONARY OF THE PERIODICAL PRESS.

OR the benefit of beginners, we append the names and addresses of some of the leading periodical publications, with a slight sketch of their character and scope. The list makes no pretension to be complete; for, while it embraces the leading journals and magazines of general interest —not forgetting even those less ambitious but widely-circulated issues to which we referred while insisting that the amateur must not shrink from a humble beginning—our narrow space necessarily excludes notice of either the provincial press, or of organs devoted to the special interests of this or that trade, society, or sect; though on these there are thousands of pens perennially and profitably at work. In the interest of the general reader, as well as of the amateur, we have, in some instances, added a few historical details about the publications named, taking conscientious care, however, that in so doing we wound no sensibility and betray no trust. In cases where personal allusion is made to editors, either their names have

already been publicly associated, in *Men of the Time* or elsewhere, with the papers they conduct, or are in all men's mouths in that connexion, or else they are used by a permission, for which, as well as for all other help and kindness afforded to us by individuals, or by publications, in the compilation of this little book, we here beg to express our cordial thanks.

Academy (52, Carey Street, Lincoln's Inn ; Weekly, 3d.), established in 1869 as a literary, artistic and scientific review, differing from the *Athenæum*, which it otherwise too closely resembles, by special prominence given to science, and by the rule that its critical notices be signed by the writers. Whether this system produces criticism that is more responsible and influential than anonymous writing need not be discussed here, but it has at any rate served to show that the *Academy* possesses a brilliant and learned staff. This staff was ably directed for some years by Dr. Appleton, whose death in 1879 cut short a promising career.

After Work (62, Paternoster Row ; Monthly, 1d.), an illustrated journal for the working classes.

All the Year Round (26, Wellington Street, Strand ; Monthly, 9d. ; Weekly, 2d.), a magazine of general literature and social politics. Established in 1859 by Charles Dickens upon the disruption of his connection with Messrs. Bradbury and Evans, the publishers of *Household Words*, which the novelist had till then conducted. His separation from his wife had occurred shortly before, and, though an entirely private matter, had given rise to much public talk. Two ladies in particular had set afloat some false rumours reflecting on Charles Dickens' domestic character. In answer to these widely-spread but idle accusations he resolved to make public a kind of manifesto headed "Personal," which duly appeared on the first page of his periodical, *Household Words :* and he requested Messrs. Bradbury and Evans to print a duplicate on the back of *Punch,* of which they were also the publishers. Those gentlemen declined on the ground of good taste, alleging that a comic journal was not the proper medium for explanations of a grave and delicate nature. From this difference of opinion resulted a separation between author and publishers ; the former established *All the Year Round,* and the latter *Once a Week,* upon the ruins of *Household Words.* Charles Dickens' journal became a noted feature of the periodical press ; it was conducted with rare liberality towards the claims of unknown aspirants, in whose contributions the conductor seemed to take a warm personal interest. The younger Charles Dickens ably edits the journal now.

Anglo-American Publications :—1. *American Traveller* (4, Langham Place, W; Weekly, 1d.), a literary, political and social newspaper, established 1874, and "devoted to the interests of Americans abroad." 2. *Anglo-American Times* (127, Strand ; Weekly, 4d.), established 1865 ; conducted on neutral principles, gives special attention to the American news of the week. 3. *Atlantic Monthly* (57, Ludgate Hill ; Monthly, 1s.), an excellent magazine of literature, science, art and politics. Excellent magazines also are *Harper's, Scribner's* and *Lippincott's,* both of which circulate largely this side of the Atlantic.

Anglo-Colonial and Anglo-European Publications :—1. *British Mail* (40, Chancery Lane ; Monthly, 2s.) 2. *European Mail* (Colonial Buildings, Cannon Street, E.C. ; price varies according to the quarter of the world to which it is sent). 3. *Foreign Times* (13, Sherborne Lane, E.C. ; Fortnightly, 2d.) 4. *Home News* (55, Parliament Street, S.W.) 5. *Overland Mail* (65, Cornhill, E.C. ; Weekly, 6d.)

Animal World (9, Paternoster Row ; Monthly, 2d.) Illustrated ; the advocate of kindness to animals.

Antiquary (62, Paternoster Row; Monthly, 1s.), a magazine "devoted to the study of the past," and edited by Mr. Edward Walford, author of "Old and New London" and a number of other well-known works, in whose hands it has become one of the most successful of the periodicals having 1880 for the year of their birth.

Architectural and Building Journals :—1. *Architect* (175, Strand; Weekly, 4d.), established 1869. A model technical paper. It contains articles of general as well as professional interest, especially on artistic and sanitary subjects. So do (2) the *British Architect and Northern Engineer* (35, Bouverie Street, Fleet Street; Weekly, 4d.), established 1874; (3) the *Builder* (46, Catherine Street, Strand; Weekly, 4d.), established 1842; (4) the *Building News* (31, Tavistock Street, W.C.; Weekly, 4d.), established 1854; and (5) the *Building World* (31, Southampton Street, Strand; Monthly, 3d.), established 1877.

Argosy (8, New Burlington Street; Monthly, 6d.), an illustrated magazine of tales, travels, essays, and verses, conducted by Mrs. Henry Wood, with the assistance of her son, Mr. Charles W. Wood.

Artist (185, Fleet Street; Monthly, 4d.), is the only newspaper of the art world published, and a very good one too.

Art Journal (26, Ivy Lane; Monthly, 2s. 6d.), an illustrated magazine founded by and inseparably connected with the name and perhaps too amiable character of Mr. Samuel Carter Hall, who, as journalist, author, and editor, has a literary history that goes back almost as far as the century. Art is in a flourishing state, at any rate pecuniarily, in England now, the artist's remuneration being of a more adequate nature than that which falls to the lot of his literary brother; and it is undoubtedly to the modern writers on art in general and to Mr. Hall in particular that the artist of to-day owes the appreciation of a wide public. When will art return the compliment, and give us representations of distressed authors which will harrow the hearts of editors and publishers, and unloose their purse-strings? Mr. Hall has recently vacated the editorial chair at the office of the *Art Journal*, where his place is taken by Mr. Marcus Huish, who, though young, has already made a position in the world of literature and art.

Art, Magazine of (Cassell, Petter, Galpin and Co., Ludgate Hill, E.C. ; Monthly, 7d.), established in 1878, and has already attained the wide popularity justly attaching to publications which are cheap but *not* nasty, light but not trivial, instructive but never dull. The scope of the magazine is indicated by its title, the editor excluding from his pages all topics except those directly connected with the Fine and the Industrial Arts.

Athenæum (20, Wellington Street, Strand ; Weekly, 3d.), a journal of literature, science, art, music, and the drama, founded in 1828 by James Silk Buckingham ; soon became the property of Charles Wentworth Dilke, father of the first and grandfather of the present baronet of that name. His talent as an editor and a critic raised the paper to the position it now holds as the leading weekly organ of the literary world— its verdict on any book under notice carrying weight not only with every bookseller and librarian in England, but also with the publishers and readers of the new world. The present Under Secretary for Foreign Affairs succeeded his father in the proprietorship of the *Athenæum*, and he also owns *Notes and Queries* and a great part of the *Gardener's Chronicle* and of the *Agricultural Gazette*. A man of marked literary ability, he is understood to have at one time edited the *Athenæum* himself ; but that task, which requires so much judgment and tact, now devolves on another. Hepworth Dixon was editor from 1853 to 1869.

Baptist Publications :—1. *Baptist* (61, Paternoster Row, E.C. ; Weekly, 1d.) 2. *Freeman* (21, Castle Street, Holborn ; Weekly, 1d.)

Bazaar, Exchange and Mart (170, Strand; Wednesday and Saturday, 2d.), an illustrated and admirably arranged medium for the exchange and sale of personal property by private persons. Also contains articles and information on practical and household subjects. Its proprietors are the representatives of the late Serjeant Cox.

Belgravia Magazine (214, Piccadilly, W.; Monthly, 1s.), established in 1866, and edited for some time by Miss Braddon, from whose hands it passed a few years ago into those of Messrs. Chatto and Windus, who have made it a very bright miscellany of light literature.

Biograph (12, Tavistock Street, Covent Garden; Monthly, 1s.), a magazine almost entirely taken up with the biographies, some of them very careful and exhaustive, of persons eminent in every kind of career. Established in 1879, and edited by Guy Roslyn.

Blackwood's Edinburgh Magazine (37, Paternoster Row, E.C.; Monthly, 2s. 6d.), during the sixty-three years of its existence has perhaps published a larger number of brilliant contributions than any other periodical of the kind. A list of those who have written in its pages would be an enumeration of nearly all the names celebrated in literature during the last half-century. *Blackwood* gives not only tales, poems, social and literary essays, but also striking political articles, with a strong Conservative bias, in spite of which, however, it scathingly criticised "Lothair."

Bow Bells (315, Strand; Weekly, 1d.) is described as a family magazine of light literature, fiction, fashion, &c. Messrs. John Dicks and George William Reynolds are the proprietors.

Brief (81, Great Queen Street, W.C.; Weekly, 2d.), an epitome of the press, resembling *Public Opinion* but more succinct both in its quotations and in its original matter, first issued by Messrs. Wyman and Sons, the great printers, in 1877. *Brief* is intended for those readers who have no time for the wordiness of the modern press.

British Quarterly Review (27, Paternoster Row; Quarterly, 6s.), a political and critical review, established in 1844, and ably conducted upon Liberal principles, the present head of the Liberal party having himself recently contributed to its pages an interesting paper upon the Evangelical origin of the Romeward movement.

Cassell's Family Magazine (Ludgate Hill, E.C.; Monthly, 7d.), a popular collection of social and domestic sketches, novels, stories, essays and poems. This periodical, like others issued by the same firm, bears the marks of the collective wisdom of the editorial board of general direction which exists in La Belle Sauvage Yard, as well as of the individual care of the one editor who has it under his especial charge. This system works well; for the principle that two heads are better than one is never more applicable than to the conduct of a magazine; and the board of general direction, which aids each editor where he requires it, includes not only men of wide literary experience and keen judgment, but men of commerce also, and the two together succeed in producing publications which are at once literary and commercial successes. By the editors of Messrs. Cassell, Petter and Galpin's magazines communications from outsiders always receive the attention they deserve.

Catholic (Roman) Publications:—1. *Catholic Fireside* (83, Fleet Street; Monthly, 2d.), an illustrated magazine of popular literature, taking the place among Catholics which is held among Protestants by the *Sunday at Home* and the *Leisure Hour*, only with a little less of the religious element; edited by the Rev. Father Nugent, the well-known Catholic Chaplain of the Liverpool Borough Gaol. 2. *Catholic Progress* (17, Portman Street, W.; Monthly, 3d.), edited by the Rev. Albany J. Christie, M.A., an Oxford convert, and a member of the Jesuit community attached to the church in Farm Street, Grosvenor Square. 3. *Catholic Times* (83, Fleet Street, and at Liverpool, where, like the *Catholic Fireside*, it is printed at the Boys' Refuge, founded by Father Nugent, the proprietor of the paper; Weekly, 1d.) 4. *Dublin Review* (17, Portman Street, London, W.; Quarterly, 6s.) has contained much memorable writing since its early days, when one of its editors, Cardinal Wiseman, contributed to its pages articles which were eagerly read at Oxford by an embryo cardinal even greater than he, then vicar of St. Mary the Virgin in the University city. Dr. W. G. Ward, another eminent Oxford convert to Catholicism, subsequently edited the *Dublin*, but on extreme lines, which were not popular with the bulk of his co-religionists, and he made a timely retirement from the editorial chair (whence he had spoken as if *ex cathedrâ* to those who shared his Ultramontane sympathies) at the very moment when the liberal-minded Leo XIII. succeeded Pius IX. in the chair of Peter. Bishop Hedley, an able writer and clear thinker, has since then conducted the *Dublin*, at the head of a staff which includes nearly all the literary talent with an ecclesiastical bias to be found in his communion. 5. *Irish Monthly* (17, Portman Street, W.; Monthly, 6d.), a bright magazine of general literature, which, edited by the Rev. Father Matthew Russell, S.J. (brother of Mr. Charles Russell, Q.C., M.P.), and largely contributed to by Miss Rosa Mulholland, who successfully tried her novice hand as a novelist under Charles Dickens in *All the Year Round*, circulates among the Catholics of England in spite of the green cover which is symbolic of its Hibernian spirit and name. 6. *Lamp* (47, Fetter Lane, E.C.; Weekly, 1d.), an illustrated miscellany of popular serial and short stories, essays, and verse; the property of an Oxford convert, the Rev. Father William Lockhart, of the Order of Charity, a member of a family that has given a great name to English literature in the biographer of Sir Walter Scott and the editor of the *Quarterly*. 7. *The Month* (17, Portman Street, W.; 2s.), founded in 1863, and edited by the Rev. Father Coleridge, S.J. (brother of the Judge), one of the ablest writers and preachers of his church. 8. *The Tablet* (27, Wellington Street, Strand; Weekly, 5d.), founded in 1840, and connected in its early history with the name of the late Frederic Lucas, M.P., one of the few men who have taken the long leap from

Quakerism to the Catholic Church. The *Tablet* is now ably edited and sub-edited by Oxford converts, one of whom was formerly a clergyman, and it may be fairly described as a Catholic (and Conservative) counterpart of the *Spectator.* 9. *Weekly Register* (44, Catherine Street, Strand; Weekly, 4d.), founded in 1849, the late Mr. Henry William Wilberforce, youngest son of the great anti-slavery reformer, being its proprietor and editor from 1854 to 1863,—"in this, as in all his undertakings" (says his friend, Cardinal Newman), "actuated by an earnest desire to promote the interests of religion, though at the sacrifice of his own." The *Register* has changed hands several times since then, being now in great part the property of Mr. De Lacy Towle. In some respects a Catholic counterpart of *The Guardian,* the *Register* is now edited by a journalist and author of long standing and distinction.

Chambers' Journal (47, Paternoster Row; Monthly, 7d.) has been celebrated for the popular and instructive character of its essays and tales for nearly half a century.

Charing Cross Magazine (5, Friar Street, Broadway, E.C.; Monthly, 6d.), of miscellaneous literature. Established in 1872.

Church of England Publications :—1. *Church Bells* (Paternoster Buildings, E.C.; Weekly, 1d.) 2. *Church Review* (11, Burleigh Street, W.C.; Weekly, 1d.) 3. *Church Times* (32, Little Queen Street, W.C.; Weekly, 1d.) The two latter are strong party newspapers, with Ritualistic views. 4. *Church and State* (Friar Street, Broadway, E.C.; Weekly, 1d.), Church of England articles, stories, essays, and reviews. 5. *Church Sunday School Magazine* (34, New Bridge Street, E.C.; Monthly, 4d.), for Sunday school teachers. 6. *Churchman's Companion* (78, New Bond Street; Monthly, 6d.), High Church; essays, reviews, and tales. Established in 1847. 7. *Churchman's Shilling Magazine and Family Treasury* (7, Paternoster Buildings, E.C.; Monthly, 1s.), religious articles, verses, reviews, &c. 8. *Church Quarterly Review* (New Street Square, E.C.; 6s.) 9. *Ecclesiastical Gazette* (13, Charing

Cross, S.W. ; Monthly, 6d. ; sent gratuitously to the leading clergy).   10.
English Churchman (2, Tavistock Street, W.C. ; Weekly, 3d.)   11. *Friendly
Leaves* (187, Piccadilly ; Monthly, 1d.), illustrated magazine for working
girls.   12. *Guardian* (5, Burleigh Street, Strand ; Wednesday, 6d.), was established in 1846 by several Oxford
men.   The story of the *Guardian*
—its early struggles, the brilliance
of its staff, the service it has done
to high Anglicanism and to political Liberalism, the distinctions won by its
proprietors—will, when written, be one of the most interesting, if not romantic,
chapters in a detailed history of journals and journalism.   An organ of which
any party may be proud, the *Guardian* is also read by outsiders, who appreciate
its excellent foreign correspondence, its carefully-arranged summary of news,
and, above all, its notices of books, which are among the very best that
appear.   Mr. Sharp is the most successful of editors, and he evidently has a
sub-editor who is worthy of his chief.   13. *John Bull* (6, Whitefriars Street,
E.C. ; Weekly, 5d.), avowedly set on foot in 1820 with the object of assail-
ing Queen Caroline and those who espoused her cause.   "On the subject of
this sickening woman," politely remarked *John Bull* in an early number, "we
shall enter into no arguments or discussions, because they go for nothing at
this period of her adventures."   The law of libel was soon made unpleasantly
familiar to the registered printers and proprietors of the lively paper, which
was edited by Theodore Hook.   He, however, disliked to be known as the
editor, and even wrote a letter to his own columns disavowing his connexion
with the paper, and at the same time published an editorial paragraph calling
attention to the disavowal, and sneering unmercifully at himself.   The success
of *John Bull* was extraordinary, its circulation amounting to 10,000 in the
sixth week of its publication.   On the death of Queen Caroline in 1821, the
occupation of the paper was gone ; and it subsequently changed its character

so far as to become, what it now is, a Church of England newspaper. 14. *Literary Churchman* (163, Piccadilly, W.; Fortnightly, 4d.), reviews of books and articles on Church topics; high in tone. 15. *Monthly Packet of Evening Readings* (6, Paternoster Row; 1s.), High Church magazine of religious and general reading. 16. *Parish Magazine* (2, Paternoster Buildings, E.C.; Monthly, 1d.), Church of England family magazine, localized in several places. 17. *Record* (1, Red Lion Court, Fleet Street; Monday, Wednesday, and Friday, 2½d.), an Evangelical journal which was once, strange to say, contributed to by his Eminence Cardinal Newman. Hence the *Record* dates back into the dim past, having been born in 1828, five years before there was any Oxford Movement to vex its soul. 18. *Rock* (Southampton Street, W.C.; Weekly, 1d.), a Low Church journal; formerly belonged to Mr. Collingridge, but recently changed hands, and has lost in the transfer some of its old spice.

Colburn's New Monthly Magazine (11, Ave Maria Lane, E.C.; Monthly, 2s. 6d.), essays, reviews, &c. Edited by Guy Roslyn.

Contemporary Review (34, Paternoster Row; Monthly, 2s. 6d.), established in 1866, and was edited for some time by Dean Alford; his place was taken in 1870 by Mr. James Knowles, whose connection with the magazine ceased seven years later. The conduct of the *Contemporary*, which is admirably arranged with a view to representing all shades of religious, political, and philosophical opinion, has since been undertaken in great part by Mr. Alexander Strahan, its publisher and proprietor.

Cornhill Magazine (15, Waterloo Place, S.W.; Monthly, 1s.), an illustrated miscellaneous magazine, started in 1860, under Thackeray's editorship, with brilliant success. It was able, being almost unique of its kind at the time, to command the foremost pens and pencils of all England. Thackeray himself,

John Ruskin, George Eliot, Elizabeth Barrett Browning, Matthew Arnold, Anthony Trollope, and Mrs. Gaskell, were among the writers, whose works were illustrated by Millais, Leighton, Fred Walker, Doyle, Du Maurier. Of the first number over 110,000 were sold. In its pages have appeared from time to time several of the classical novels of the day, and some of the best essays. Under the conduct of Mr. Leslie Stephen, the son-in-law of the first editor, the magazine has kept up its old prestige, with the addition, perhaps, of a little more cultivation of modern "aestheticism." Thackeray's tradition of liberality has been followed uniformly in the *Cornhill's* dealings with its contributors.

Country and Sporting Publications :—1. *Agricultural Economist* (47, Millbank Street, Westminster; Weekly, 6d.) 2. *Bell's Life in London* (9, Catherine Street, Strand; Weekly, 4d.) 3. *Bell's Weekly Messenger* (26, Catherine Street, Strand; Weekly, 6d.) 4. *Country* (170, Strand; Weekly, 3d.) 5. *Country Gentleman's Magazine* (13A, Salisbury Square, Fleet Street; Monthly, 1s.) 6. *Farmer* (13A, Salisbury Square, Fleet Street; Weekly, 5d.) 7. *Field* (346, Strand; Weekly, 6d.), established in 1864; one of the fine newspaper properties which Serjeant Cox left behind him. 8. *Fishing Gazette* (11, Ave Maria Lane, E.C.; Weekly, 2d.) 9. *Floral Magazine* (5, Henrietta Street, W.C.; Monthly, 3s. 6d.) 10. *Floral World* (Groombridge and Sons, Paternoster Row; Monthly, 6d.) 11. *Garden* (37, Southampton Street, W.C.; Weekly, 6d.) 12. *Gardener* (37, Paternoster Row; Monthly, 6d.) 13. *Gardener's Chronicle* (41, Wellington Street, W.C.; Weekly, 5d.) 14. *Gardener's Magazine* (11, Ave Maria Lane, E.C.; Weekly, 2d.) 15. *Horticultural Record* (317, Strand; Weekly, 1d.) 16. *Illustrated Sporting and Dramatic News* (148, Strand; Weekly, 6d.), founded in 1873, and belonged at one time to Mr. Ingram, of the *Illustrated London News.* 17. *Journal of Horticulture* (171, Fleet Street; Weekly, 3d.) 18. *Land and Water* (176, Fleet Street; Weekly, 6d.), an entertaining paper, the fishing and natural history department of which is conducted by Mr. Frank Buckland.

19. *Magnet* (19, Exeter Street, W.C.; Weekly, 3½d.) 20. *Referee* (17, Wine Office Court, Fleet Street; Weekly, 1d.), an exceedingly smartly written journal of sport, politics, and the drama. 21. *Sporting Gazette and Agricultural Journal* (135, Strand; Weekly, 4d.), started in 1862; contains portraits of sporting celebrities. 22. *Sporting Life* (148, Fleet Street; Wednesday and Saturday, 1d.) 23. *Sporting Opinion* (61, Fleet Street; Monday, 1d.) 24. *Sporting Times* (52, Fleet Street; Weekly, 2d.) 25. *Sportsman* (Boy Court, Ludgate Hill; on Saturday, 3d.; on other days, 2d.)

Court Circular (2, Southampton Street, Strand; Weekly, 5d.), was started in 1856, as a rival of the *Court Journal.* Its first editor was Mr. H. Prendergast; and a little more than ten years after its first appearance it was sold to Mr. Edward Walford, who, after editing it for a short time, re-sold it to Mr. W. H. Stephens.

Court Journal (36, Tavistock Street, W.C.; Weekly, 5d.), an occasionally illustrated record of Court and fashion, which has existed since 1829.

Daily Chronicle (Salisbury Square, Fleet Street; 1d.) This paper was established as the *Clerkenwell News* in 1855, under which title it was continued until Mr. Lloyd (of *Lloyd's Weekly News*) purchased it, and issued it daily under its new designation, no longer as a local organ, but as a Liberal paper for the public in general. The success attending the transition has been great, and Mr. Lloyd has now two fine newspaper properties instead of one.

Daily News (Bouverie Street, E.C.; Daily, 1d.) had the distinction of being introduced to the world, in 1846, by Charles Dickens as its first editor. Among its proprietors were Messrs. Bradbury and Evans, Sir William Jackson, M.P., Sir Joseph Paxton, and Sir Joshua Walmsley; its manager was Mr. Charles Wentworth Dilke, the member for Chelsea's grandfather; and among its prominent writers—who were all very handsomely remunerated—were John Forster, Harriet Martineau (one of the very few ladies who have written political leaders), and Mr. M'Cullagh Torrens, Finsbury's M.P.

Charles Dickens did not make a good editor for a daily, and the chair he vacated after an occupancy of only a few months was subsequently filled by John Forster, and then by Knight Hunt, author of "The Fourth Estate." During the first years of its existence the *Daily News* was published at great pecuniary sacrifice—successive changes in its price from 5d. to 2½d., from 2½d. to 3d., and back again to 5d. proving ineffectual to transform losses into profits. As a penny paper the *Daily News* has found its right field, and fulfilled its mission; it is now not only a literary but also a commercial success. Its circulation is known to have largely increased since the General Election, political papers being always benefited by their own party's tenure of power. The present editor, Mr. Frank Harrison Hill, was formerly a leader-writer on its staff, and is well-known as a political writer. Mr. J. R. Robinson may claim to share with Mr. Hill the credit attaching to the conduct of the *Daily News;* for it is largely to his great qualities as a manager that the prestige of the paper is due. He it is who has gathered men like Archibald Forbes (whose accompanying autograph the reader may well imagine to have been penned amid the heat and hurry of a battle) and W. H. Lucy (who writes the Parliamentary summary for its columns) round the office in Bouverie Street. Among the present proprietors of the *Daily News* are Sir Charles Reed, Mr. Samuel Morley, and Mr. Labouchere, the latter being the Besieged Resident who contributed to its columns a graphic account of Paris during the Commune.

Daily Telegraph (135, Fleet Street ; Daily, 1d.), started in 1855 by Colonel

Sleigh, who had the bad luck which is almost the rule in the case of the founders of new papers. After running the *Daily Telegraph and Courier* (as it was then called) at only twopence (an unprecedented price in those days) until he could run it no longer, the Colonel resigned it into the hands of Mr. Levy, one of his creditors. It is said to have been a toss up with Mr. Levy whether he should take the paper—a toss up, that is, whether he would or would not make himself the master of a magnificent fortune. For the *Telegraph* prospered under new management. The advertisements in its columns then brought in a daily revenue of 7/6, but now they bring, according to Mr. Grant, a sum of about £500; and the literary scope and excellence of the paper has increased in like proportion. One of Mr. Levy's early acts was to halve the price of the *Telegraph*, which made a sensation by supplying for a penny a double sheet similar to that for which the *Times* charged fourpence. The abolition of the paper duty added to the profits of the new daily many thousands of pounds a year, and also enabled the proprietors to print on better material than before. The circulation of the *Telegraph* is the largest in the world; its social, chatty articles giving it a charm for the general reader. Largely contributed to by the king of journalists, Mr. George Augustus Sala, the *Telegraph* is conducted by Mr. Edward L. Lawson, aided by Mr. Edwin Arnold, C.S.I., and a well organized staff.

Day of Rest (34, Paternoster Row, E.C. ; Monthly, 6d.), general literature for Sunday reading. Describes itself as " Unsectarian," a term which, in the case of several publications (perhaps the *Day of Rest* is one of them), would often mislead High Anglicans or Catholics who supposed it meant toleration for any theology which was not either Low or Broad.

Echo (22, Catherine Street, W.C. ; Evening, ½d.), founded by Messrs. Cassell, Petter & Galpin in 1868, edited by Mr. Arthur Arnold, now member for Salford, and sub-edited by Mr. G. Barnett Smith, an able and industrious *littérateur*. Mr. J. Passmore Edwards, M.P., now owns the *Echo* and edits it with *verve*.

Economist (340, Strand, W.C.; Weekly, 3d.), a journal of commerce, mining, political economy, &c., established in 1843.

Edinburgh Review (39, Paternoster Row; Quarterly, 6s.), established in 1802, under circumstances which everyone remembers. Jeffrey, Brougham, Macaulay, had talent enough between them to produce a publication that was striking and readable enough in its day, though the absence of current interest makes a perusal of the great bulk of its articles in the old numbers a trifle tedious now. How Brougham was jealous of all his fellow contributors, especially disliking Macaulay, whom he called the biggest bore in London, and how Macaulay reciprocated the hostile feeling, is all told in the correspondence of Macvey Napier, editor of the *Edinburgh* for many years, and is not one of the pleasantest chapters in literary history. In this quarterly, as in its great Tory rival, the articles are always headed by the title of a book, or of a number of books; but one occasionally suspects that one is really perusing an original essay rather than a review. In fact, Macaulay owned that he ignored his author when, in devoting a hundred pages of the *Edinburgh* to what purported to be a notice of the "Memoirs of the Life of Warren Hastings, by the Reverend G. R. Gleig," he introduced an eloquent disquisition on Indian history with the candid avowal, "We are inclined to think that we shall best meet the wishes of our readers if, instead of dwelling upon the faults of this book, we attempt to give our own view of the life and character of Mr. Hastings;" nor does Mr. Gleig's name appear more than three times in the whole paper. The *Edinburgh* has been edited for nearly a quarter of a century by Mr. Henry Reeve, C.B., the eminent *littérateur*, to whom Charles Greville confided his celebrated "Journal" for publication.

Educational Publications :—1. *Educational Times* (1, Gough Square, E.C.;

F

Monthly, 6d.) 2. *Scholastic World* (1, Wine Office Court, Fleet Street; Monthly, 2d.) 3. *School Board Chronicle* (72, Turnmill St., E.C.; Weekly, 3d.), the organ of the School Boards, edited by Mr. R. Gowing, formerly editor of *Gentleman's Magazine*. 4. *Schoolmaster* (14, Red Lion Court; Weekly, 1d.)

Examiner (136, Strand; Weekly, 3d.) has a notable history, both literary and political, which dates back nearly to the beginning of the century. When Leigh Hunt edited the paper, Byron and Shelley were interestingly connected with it, the latter declaring that his poems were not thought good enough by Leigh Hunt to be printed there! The *Examiner*, long the property of Mr. Peter Taylor, the Radical M.P., has recently changed hands more than once, and has also halved its price. Both the *Examiner* and *Life* are under the editorial direction of Mr. Charles Williams, who has done good work as a war correspondent, and in other walks of his profession.

Family Herald (421, Strand; Weekly, 1d.), an old-established journal of popular tales and essays.

Family Reader (300, Strand; Weekly, 1d.), an illustrated miscellany of stories and essays.

Fortnightly Review (193, Piccadilly; Monthly, 2s. 6d.), ably edited by Mr. John Morley, a Radical in politics and a Positivist in religion.

Fraser's Magazine (39, Paternoster Row; Monthly, 2s. 6d.), political and social essays; lately edited by W. Allingham, and now by Principal Tulloch.

Freemason (198, Fleet Street; Weekly, 2d.)

Freemason's Chronicle (67, Barbican, E.C.; Weekly, 3d.)

Fun (153, Fleet Street ; Weekly, 1d.), established in 1860, and, in its illustration department, especially memorable for the drawings of Mr. Sullivan.

Funny Folks (Red Lion Court, Fleet Street ; Weekly, 1d.), edited by Mr. William Sawyer, who has written much and well in prose and verse.

Genealogist (55, Great Russell Street, W.C. ; Quarterly, 2s. 6d.)

Gentleman's Magazine (214, Piccadilly ; Monthly, 1s.) has a splendid history, dating from 1731, about which a volume might be written. It has altered its character of late years, and no longer contains that chronicle of contemporary events which makes the back volumes so valuable now, but is wholly occupied with high-class general literature.

Globe (110, Strand ; Evening, 1d.), started in 1802 by the London publishers, who considered themselves uncivilly treated by the *Morning Post*, then their principal advertising medium. The John Murray of that day was one of its great supporters ; but the paper's want of success soon led to the falling away of most of the publishers, and Mr. Lane, the manager, had an almost lonely struggle before he put the *Globe* upon a commercially sound basis. With the *Globe* has been incorporated the *Traveller*, and several other evening papers, which were obliged to relinquish a separate existence. For the first sixty years of its issue the *Globe* was a Liberal paper, and its change to the other political side caused as much comment as the recent and contrary transition of the *Pall Mall*. Once upon a time a past editor of the *Globe* had a furious controversy with D'Israeli the younger ; but the Lord Beaconsfield of to-day has few more able and sincere admirers than the editor and staff of the pink sheet.

Good Words (56, Ludgate Hill ; Monthly, 6d.), a magazine of literature, fiction, essays, poetry, &c., which has a large circulation, and which remunerates its distinguished writers with marked liberality. It is edited by Dr. McLeod, who is substantially assisted in that task by Mr. Alexander H. Japp—himself a delightful writer. *Good Words*, as its name would imply, is strongly tinged with religion, and is intended to supply Sunday reading to those pious households which are yet not so strict as to taboo the secular interest of Mr. Black's novels (Mr. Black has been a busy journalist in his day), and of briskly-written sketches of travel and adventure.

Graphic (190, Strand; Weekly, 6d.) divides with the *Illustrated London News* a particular field of illustrated journalism, and is planned upon much the same lines as its contemporary and competitor. The latter, until the *Graphic* started, had had no rival except the *Illustrated Times*, which was short-lived, in spite of its excellent letterpress. Our business being here entirely with the literary part of the paper, we will say nothing of the engravings, which (under the management of Mr. Thomas) are, of course, its distinguishing feature. Its tone is decidedly light; its articles are chatty and of the widest range; it contains batches of paragraphs upon the current topics of the day, *vers de société*, and a quantity of attractive scraps of all kinds. It is not closed to the efforts of aspiring outsiders. The *Graphic*, edited by Mr. Arthur Locker, brother of the author of the popular "London Lyrics," and himself a poet, has succeeded brilliantly from its first number, both here and in America, whither it is regularly sent in stereotype to be reprinted there.

Hand and Heart (1, Paternoster Buildings, E.C.; Weekly, 1d.), a popular "journal of news and entertaining literature."

House and Home (335, Strand; Weekly, 1d.), an occasionally illustrated journal of sanitation, house improvement, and domestic economy.

Illustrated London News (198, Strand; Weekly, 6d.), founded in 1842 by Mr. Ingram, who—like his son, the present proprietor of the paper—represented Boston in Parliament. At first a struggling enterprise, at times almost parted with in despair for a trifling sum, the *Illustrated* developed into a splendid property. It is no hyperbole to say that it is known wherever the English language is spoken, and that it circulates with the sun. Its letter-press combines the solid and the light; it often contains art criticism of quite unusual excellence, and Mr. Sala's altogether distinctive pen has lately brightened its pages with paragraphs on the current topics of the week.

Jewish Publications:—1. *Jewish Chronicle* (43, Finsbury Square; Weekly, 2d.) 2. *Jewish World* (8, South Street, Finsbury; Weekly, 1d.)

Judy (73, Fleet Street; Weekly, 2d.), an illustrated humorous journal.

Juvenile publications of all kinds exist in such enormous numbers that we excuse ourselves from making a list of them here; the more willingly because they are so low in price that an amateur ordering a shilling's-worth at his bookseller's will obtain a bundle of such publications, and be able to examine the character of their columns before becoming a candidate for a place in them.

Kensington (11, Stationers' Hall Court, E.C.; Monthly, 6d.), a literary magazine and review, edited by Mrs. Leith Adams.

Ladies' Publications:—1. *Englishwoman's Domestic Magazine* (Dorset Buildings, Salisbury Square, E.C.; Monthly, 1s.), illustrated miscellany of literature, fashions, and needlework. 2. *Englishwoman's Review of Social and Industrial Questions* (57, Ludgate Hill; Monthly, 6d.), advocates the advancement of women. 3. *Ladies' Treasury and Treasury of Literature* (10, Paternoster Buildings, E.C.; Monthly, 6d.), literature, domestic economy, and fashion. 4. *Myra's Journal of Dress and Fashion* (40, Bedford Street, W.C.; Monthly, 3d.) 5. *Queen* (346, Strand; Weekly, 6d.), a large and singularly complete ladies' newspaper; one of the splendid journalistic properties of the late Serjeant Cox, and now owned by his representatives. It frequently contains ably-written articles, and a capital collection of general news, so that it is by no means despised by the husbands and fathers and brothers of its subscribers. In its feminine departments—presided over by a most able editress, under whose conduct the paper has risen to its present eminent position—it is at once practical, artistic, housewifely, and millinerial. 6. *Sylvia's Home Journal* (Dorset Buildings, Salisbury Square, E.C. ; Monthly, 6d.), a ladies' journal of tales, stories, patterns, and fashions. 7. *Woman's Gazette, or News about Work* (187, Piccadilly, W. ; Monthly, 2d.), advocates the advancement and employment of woman. 8. *Young Ladies' Journal* (135, Salisbury Square, E.C. ; Weekly, 1d.), fashions, needlework, and tales.

Legal Publications:—1. *Law Journal* (5, Quality Court, Chancery Lane ; Weekly, 6d.) 2. *Law Times* (10, Wellington Street, W.C. ; Weekly, 1s.), was the property of the late Serjeant Cox.

Leisure Hour (56, Paternoster Row ; Monthly, 6d.), a well-conducted illustrated magazine of stories and popular essays for family reading.

Life (136, Strand ; Weekly, 6d.), one of the society papers, started in 1879, and soon distinguished by the pretty phototype reproductions of fair faces, generally drawn by Frank Miles, and of Continental pictures. Mr. R. Davey, a journalist with a reputation on both sides the Atlantic, was in a sense the literary father of *Life*, but it was eventually produced under the editorial care of Mr. H. P. Stephens. The paper was recently transferred from its first proprietors to the owner of the *Examiner*, and both papers are conducted under the same roof.

Literary World (13, Fleet Street ; Weekly, 1d.), a popular journal of literature, containing notices of books, and articles of literary interest.

Lloyd's Weekly London Newspaper (12, Salisbury Square, Fleet St. ; Sunday, 1d.), a Liberal paper for the people. The editorial chair left vacant in

1857 by the death of Douglas Jerrold was filled by his son, Mr. Blanchard Jerrold, who has written much for the *Daily News*, the *Morning Post*, the *Gentleman's Magazine*, the *Athenæum*, and is also the author of many well-known works.

London Figaro (35, St. Bride St., E.C.; Weekly, 1d.), a smartly-written political, critical, and satirical journal, edited by Mr. J. Mortimer, who was recently imprisoned for publishing Mrs. Weldon's statements about certain domestic affairs.

London Journal (332, Strand; Weekly, 1d.), a miscellany of fiction and popular papers, established in 1845.

London Reader (334, Strand; Weekly, 1d.), an illustrated journal of light literature.

London Society (188, Fleet Street; Monthly, 1s.), a magazine of general literature, lately edited by Florence Marryat, and now by Mr. Hogg; it is the lightest of the shilling monthlies, for while the others always introduce more or less solid padding into their numbers, *London Society* frankly eschews everything that is not amusing.

Macmillan's Magazine (29, Bedford Street, Covent Garden; Monthly, 1s.), since its foundation in 1859, has contained stories and essays of great merit. Edited by Mr. Grove, who succeeded Professor 'David Masson, *Macmillan's* takes a high literary place among its contemporaries, which are also in a sense its imitators.

Manufacturing and Mechanical Publications :—1. *Design and Work* (41, Tavistock Street, W.C.; Weekly, 2d.) 2. *Engineer* (163, Strand; Weekly, 6d.) 3. *Engineering and Building Times* (125, Fleet St.; Weekly, 2d.) 4. *English Mechanic and World of Science* (31, Tavistock St., W.C.; Weekly, 2d.) 5. *Iron* (12, Fetter Lane, E.C.; Weekly, 6d.)

Medical Publications:—*British Medical Journal* (161A, Strand; Weekly, 6d.), official organ of the British Medical Association. 2. *Health* (Sheffield Street, Lincoln's Inn; Monthly, 1d.), family magazine of sanitary and social interest. 3. *Herald of Health* (429, Oxford Street; Monthly, 1d.), magazine of sanitary and social science. Edited by Dr. T. L. Nichols, who, besides being a successful author, has done journalistic work as London correspondent of a New York paper, and in other ways. 4. *Homœopathic World* (2, Finsbury Circus, E.C.; Monthly, 6d.) 5. *Journal of Mental Science* (11, New Burlington Street, W.; Quarterly, 3s. 6d.), organ of the Medico-Psychological Association. 6. *Lancet* (423, Strand; Weekly, 7d.), the leading organ of the medical profession. 7. *Medical Times and Gazette* (11, New Burlington Street, W.; Weekly, 6d.) 8. *Monthly Homœopathic Review* (59, Moorgate Street, E.C.; 1s.)

Methodist Publications:—1. *Methodist* (317, Strand; Weekly, 1d.) 2. *Methodist Recorder* (161, Fleet St.; Weekly, 1d.) 3. *Primitive Methodist* (4, Wine Office Court, Fleet St.; Weekly, 1d.) 4. *Watchman* (161, Fleet St.; Weekly, 3d.)

Morning Advertiser (127, Fleet Street; Daily, 3d.), the organ of the Licensed Victuallers; it was established in 1794 by a society of that fraternity, every member agreeing to take in the paper daily, and each member to be entitled to a share in the profits. Down to 1850 the paper circulated only among publicans and the lower class of coffee-house keepers; but at that date an effort was made to extend its operations. The paper was enlarged and improved, and a circulation of under 5,000 copies grew in four years until it was nearly doubled, and the 1,500 or 1,600 proprietors were dividing a profit of £12,000 a year. The late Mr. James Grant was for many years editor of the *Morning Advertiser*, and which was at one time contributed to by Lord Brougham.

Morning Post (12, Wellington St., W.C. ; Daily, 3d.), a political, general and fashionable newspaper; was founded so long ago as 1772, and when first issued was the size of one sheet of the *Pall Mall Gazette* of to-day. At one period in its history the paper was owned in part by the Prince Regent, whose breakfast-table literature at Carlton House, according to one of our poets, consisted of "Death warrants and the *Morning Post.*" Its writers in the past have included Charles Lamb, Southey, Sir James Mackintosh, Wordsworth, Tom Moore, Praed and Coleridge, the latter being one of successive and successful editors. When the venerable paper celebrated its centenary on Nov. 2nd, 1872, it devoted several columns to a most interesting account of its own history. With Sir Algernon Borthwick for its present proprietor and editor, and with an able staff at his side, the *Post* maintains its old prestige, and never carried more weight with its political, social, and literary verdicts than it does now.

Music :—1. *Musical Standard* (185, Fleet Street ; Weekly, 3d.) 2. *Musical Times* (1, Berners Street, W. ; Monthly, 3d.) 3. *Musical World* (244, Regent Street ; Weekly, 4d.)

Nature (29, Bedford Street, Strand ; Weekly, 6d.) deals with scientific discoveries and books. Published by Messrs. Macmillan & Co., and edited by Dr. J. Norman Lockyer, *Nature* is quite the best organ for the class of readers for whom it is particularly designed.

Nineteenth Century (1, Paternoster Square ; Monthly, 2s. 6d.), founded and edited by Mr. James Knowles, an able man, who was formerly an architect, having built, among other places, the Surrey residence of Mr. Alfred Tennyson, his great friend and the contributor to his periodical. Mr. Knowles formerly edited the *Contemporary*, which the *Nineteenth Century* resembles in its general scope ;

F 2

and he originated in 1869 the Metaphysical Society, whose members reflected the most various phases of current thought. As its name implies, the *Nineteenth Century* is intended to be in every way of its time; it allows the principal intellectual battles (especially the theological and anti-theological controversy) to be fought out in its arena without fear or favour. Every one of its articles, it may be added, is signed by a name of some note.

Nonconformist (13, Fleet Street; Weekly, 6d.), a paper that embodies the best traditions of Liberalism and Nonconformity, is conscientiously conducted, and often has exceptionally discriminating notices of books.

Notes and Queries (20, Wellington Street, W.C.; Weekly, 4d.) contains antiquarian, literary, scientific and artistic memoranda and information, chiefly contributed by outside correspondents.

Observer (396, Strand; Sunday, 4d.), a political, social and literary newspaper with a history which goes back as far as 1791, and at no period of which was it in a better position than it is now.

Pall Mall Budget (6d.) is a weekly collection of articles printed in the *Pall Mall Gazette*, with a summary of news.

Pall Mall Gazette (2, Northumberland Street, Strand; Every Evening, 2d.), established in 1865 by Mr. George Smith, head of the firm of Smith, Elder, and Co., as proprietor, and Mr. Frederick Greenwood as editor. Several thousand pounds were spent, in announcing its advent and otherwise, at its inception, and it paid its contributors munificently. In spite of this expenditure, and the high standing the paper took from the first, it proved an unprofitable enterprise for many years. James Greenwood's first "Amateur Casual" article (for which he received 100 guineas) drew the *Pall Mall* into a more general popularity; but, notwithstanding, serious changes in the paper were deemed necessary, the price being lowered from twopence to a penny—and without any success. The next experiment was to publish, in 1870, a morning as well as an evening edition of the *Pall Mall*, and the experiment spelled ruin. The first form was then recurred to and is still retained, the paper having become a fine property in the meantime. The political history of the *Pall Mall* is well known, and has lately been the subject of great comment. Only a few weeks after Mr. Gladstone, then in opposition, had confessed that the *Pall Mall* was his most able arraigner in the press, the public was surprised to hear that the same statesman, having regained office, was in a position to compliment the very same evening journal, "written by gentlemen for gentlemen," on being no longer his keenest foe, but his kindest friend. The fact was that Mr. Smith had transferred the paper to his son-in-law, Mr. Henry Yates Thompson, to whom, a Liberal, its political independence was not acceptable. The change of proprietorship necessitated a change in the editorial department also, Mr. Greenwood resigning a post he could no longer conscientiously retain, not without a keen and natural regret in parting from a paper which he "planned, down to the little details of paper and type," which are so dear to the journalistically paternal mind. Mr. F. W. Joynes, the principal sub-editor of the paper from its foundation till 1880, retired with his chief, also some members of the staff.

Pan (4, Lugdate Circus Buildings, E.C. ; Weekly, 6d.), a satirical journal, edited by Mr. Alfred Thompson, whose only enemies will be "unjust, corrupt, and cruel men, pretenders, upstarts, snobs, and humbugs."

Pen (22, Tavistock Street, Covent Garden, W.C.; Monthly, 6d.) This was originally started, in the spring of 1880, as a weekly two-penny literary paper, differing from those already established by giving an exclusive attention to literary subjects ; also by the reproduction of drawings from the illustrated books under review; and by the light articles and paragraphs which popularized its pages. In their prospectus, the projectors of the *Pen* stated their belief that "the best and most difficult function of the critic is the discovery of merits rather than of defects;" and promised "that while we shall praise nothing that is not good for the sake of being pleasant, we shall never be tempted into injustice for the mere sake of being smart." Under new management, the *Pen* now appears as a monthly, not exclusively devoted to criticism and news, but with an admixture of fiction, travels, etc.

Penny Illustrated Paper (10, Milford Lane, Strand ; Weekly, 1d.)

Phonetic Journal (20, Paternoster Row, E.C.; Weekly, 1d.), Mr. Pitman's organ of the Phonetic Society.

Pictorial World (63, Fleet Street; Weekly, 2d.), an illustrated family and general newspaper.

Portfolio (54, Fleet Street ; Monthly, 2s. 6d.), a high-class art journal, to be prized equally for its illustrations and its letterpress. Edited by Philip Hamerton, the *Portfolio* cannot fail to be charming ; and it also presents to amateurs a fair field with no favour, as may be seen from the announcement : "The editor desires to correct an impression that he accepts contributions only from writers of established reputation. He will be most willing to give room to any writer of real ability, whether he happens to be celebrated or not." A liberal decree, from which Mr. Knowles of the *Nineteenth Century* would certainly dissent.

Public Opinion (11, Southampton Street, Strand ; Weekly, 2d.), one of the happy thoughts of journalism. A collection, week by week, of the differing opinions of the home and continental press upon the events of the time ; is as amusing as it is valuable. When the paper was in its youth, its compilers combined their quotations with a piquant effect of antithesis and mutual contradiction, which seems now to be less considered. Original book-reviews and a column of correspondence, kept up with considerable briskness, are mingled with the quoted matter, which is excellently selected and arranged.

Punch (85, Fleet Street ; Weekly, 3d.) has played since 1841 a considerable part in the political and social life of England. Its literary history is well known. Editorially associated during recent years with the grave name of

Tom Taylor, its columns have been
lightened by the incomparable writings
of Mr. F. C. Burnand ; while the drawings of Mr. du Maurier have further
helped its pages to retain their hold on the public affection. *Punch* is no believer
in the old maxim that the labourer is worthy of his hire, for it every week
declares that the editor does not undertake to pay for any outside contributions
he may accept—an announcement which, in the interests of the amateur,
and for the credit of the profession, we own that we shall be glad to see
withdrawn.

Quarterly Review (50, Albemarle Street, W. ; 6s.) has a history too well
known to need recapitulation here. The present occupant of the editorial
chair, in which Gifford and Lockhart formerly sat, is Dr. William Smith, of
Classical Dictionary fame, and otherwise a man of high literary distinction.

Queen (see Ladies' Publications).

Quiver (Ludgate Hill, E.C. ; Monthly, 6d.), a magazine of Sunday reading ;
as popular and successful as everything of Messrs. Cassell, Petter, Galpin, and
Co.'s appears to be.

Religious Publications :—1. *Christian Age* (107, Fleet Street ; Weekly, 1d.)
2. *Christian Globe* (29, Farringdon Street, E.C. ; Weekly, 1d.) 3. *Christian
Herald* (2, Ivy Lane, E.C. ; Weekly, 1d.) 4. *Christian Union* (8, Salisbury
Square, Fleet Street ; Weekly, 1d.) 5. *Christian World* (13, Fleet Street ;
Weekly, 1d.)

Reynolds' Weekly Newspaper (313, Strand ; Weekly, 1d.) advocates
Republican principles.

St. James's Gazette (Dorset Street, Fleet Street ; Evening, 2d.), the paper
founded by Mr. Frederick Greenwood after his secession from the *Pall Mall
Gazette.* The new organ, which resembles the *Pall Mall* in outward
appearance. and in its style differs from it only by being a little more jaunty,
made its *début* on May 31st, 1880. Backed by a large amount of capital, read

by independent politicians and by Conservatives, written and edited with character and talent, the *St. James's Gazette* has been born with a silver spoon in its mouth, and can hardly miss a prosperous career.

St. James's Magazine and United Empire Review (5, Friar Street, Broadway, E.C.; Monthly, 1s.) novels, essays, political and biographical articles.

Saturday Review (38, Southampton Street, Strand; Weekly, 6d.), established in 1855; connected in its proprietary with the name of Mr. Beresford-Hope, M.P., and edited for some time by the late Mr. Cook. In many respects a unique-paper; its very name has acquired a flavour of its own upon the tongue—a taste of bitter herbs, astringent and not ungrateful. Yet the *Saturday Review* is at least as remarkable for its liberal recognition of merits as for its scorn of faults. It knows, indeed, how to use ridicule; and if that weapon is a legitimate, nay, valuable one, it is well that it should be employed intelligently. The tone of the paper is strongly pronounced for morality and for reverence towards the things which are generally accepted as sacred. It has never occupied the now common neutral ground of absolute indifference to all save "art" and "honour"; it is scholarly, making, perhaps, a specialty of historical and classical knowledge. The political articles lead off, followed by papers of social and other current subjects of interest in smaller type, these being succeeded by book reviews, in the course of which one author is generally crushed in each number. Periodical notices of German, American, and other foreign publications are a marked feature of the *Saturday Review.* There is no political or other trimming in its columns. It has lately stung Mr. Gladstone into a hot retort; but Lord Beaconsfield, in past years, felt the same lash, wielded, in his case, by the Marquis of Salisbury, who then increased by his pen the income of a younger son.

Service Publications:—1. *Army and Navy Gazette* (16, Wellington Street, W.C.; Weekly, 6d.), edited by Dr. W. H. Russell, the famous correspondent of *The Times* and the *Telegraph.* 2. *Broad Arrow* (2, Waterloo Place,

S.W. ; Weekly, 6d.) 3. *Civil Service Gazette* (6, Salisbury Street, Strand ; Weekly, 3d.) 4. *Colburn's United Service Magazine* (13, Great Marlborough Street ; Monthly, 3s. 6d.) 5. *Naval Chronicle* (18, Adam Street, Strand ; Monthly, 6d.) 6. *Naval and Military Gazette* (4, Spring Gardens, Charing Cross ; Weekly, 3d.) 7. *United Service Gazette* (7, Wellington Street, W.C. ; Weekly, 6d.) 8. *Volunteer Service Gazette* (121, Fleet Street ; Weekly, 4d.)

Social Notes (16, Southampton Street, Strand ; Weekly, 1d.) Articles on social reforms, requirements, and progress ; founded by the Marquis Townshend, with Mr. S. C. Hall for first editor, his sorrowful experiences in that capacity being chronicled in our law-court reports.

Society (84, Fleet Street ; Weekly, 1d.), a gossipy, bright little paper, in some ways the most wonderful pennyworth among the weeklies.

Spectator (1, Wellington Street, Strand ; Weekly, 6d.) has celebrated its golden jubilee, but shows no sign of the decrepitude of age. Mr. R. H. Hutton here mounts his pulpit every Saturday, with utterances of entire honesty, which give to his paper a singular interest and charm. Independent, outspoken, and powerful in its political articles, the *Spectator* in its literary notices is discriminating, candid, and fair ; and all its utterances on religion are marked by a freedom from bias rare indeed in any newspaper, and characteristic, like the other features of the journal, of Mr. Hutton's own mind.

Spiritualist Publications :—1. *Medium and Daybreak* (15, Southampton Row, Holborn ; Weekly, 1½d.) 2. *Spiritualist* (11, Ave Maria Lane, E.C. ; Weekly, 2d.)

Standard (104, Shoe Lane, E.C.; Morning and Evening, 1d.) was originally
an evening paper only, and was specially designed to oppose the application of
the principles of civil and religious liberty to the case of the Roman Catholics
then in England.   Dr. Giffard, an ultra-Protestant, was its first editor.
Appearing in 1827, it was soon afterwards referred to by the *Morning Chronicle*
as "a journal which has crawled into existence, and is fast hastening towards
dissolution." The *Morning Chronicle* itself fulfilled the amiable prediction it
had ventured in regard to a contemporary which, after some early struggles,
soon attained stability.   When the Maynooth Grant was placed on the Con-
solidated Fund, the *Standard*, according to Mr. James Grant, modified its
hostility to the Catholic religion at the instance of Sir Robert Peel, who took
the precaution of influencing Dr. Giffard in favour of the measure before he
introduced it in the House ; and by its desertion of the ultra-Protestant cause
on this occasion it offended many of those who had previously given it a
warm support.   The *Standard* long ago gave evidence of that honourable mode
of conducting political controversy for which it has lately been much com-
mended, refusing, as it did, to make common cause with its Tory contemporaries
against the Liberal administration in connection with the case of the Hon. Mrs.
Norton and Lord Melbourne, who was then Premier.   The *Standard*, after
it was an established success, passed from the hands of Mr. Edward Baldwin
(son of its first proprietor) into those of Mr. Johnstone, who reduced the price
from 4d. to 2d., and made it a morning as well as an evening paper.   This was
in 1857 ; and in 1858 its price was further lowered to 1d., though its size was
increased.   The *Standard* is one of the largest of the penny papers, and, perhaps
on this account, carries off the palm as to the variety and completeness of its
news.   The *Evening Standard* is published under the same auspices and at
the same place as the morning issue, which it resembles in general excellence.

Statist (16, York St., W.C.; Weekly, 6d.), financial and commercial statistics and articles.

Sunday at Home (56, Paternoster Row; Weekly, 1d.), family reading, carefully selected, and well illustrated.

Sunday Magazine (56, Ludgate Hill; Monthly, 6d.), stories, essays, verses, for Sunday and general reading.

Sunday Times (8, New Bridge St., E.C.; 2d.) A capital paper.

Temple Bar Magazine (8, New Burlington Street, W.; Monthly, 1s.), established in 1860 close upon the great success of the *Cornhill,* and laid upon much the same lines, save that it eschewed illustrations, and made a specialty of a light and journalistic style of essay, as was to be expected from the peculiar talents of its first editor, Mr. Sala. Its novels, too, were distinctively of the smart order, and this tradition it has preserved until now, by publishing some of the briskest stories by the lady novelists most in vogue. A thoroughly readable magazine, and its past numbers contain, among more ephemeral matter, some memorable articles and poems.

Theatrical Publications :—1. *Era* (49, Wellington Street, W.C.; Weekly, 5d.), founded in 1837; owned and ably conducted by Mr. Edward Ledger. 2. *Theatre* (26, Wellington Street, W.C.; Monthly, 1s.), edited by Clement Scott, the dramatic critic of the *Daily Telegraph.*

Times (Printing House Square, E.C.; Daily, 3d.) "Madam, have you seen Mr. Cambridge's excellent verses called 'The Progress of Liberty?' They appeared in a paper called *The Times* "—so wrote Horace Walpole to the Countess of Ossory on the 12th of December, 1789. From "a paper called *The Times*" to "the Leading Organ" is a long jump, and the story of it will, no doubt, be one day worthily written. Here is only space for little more than a few names and dates. First published in 1785, under the title of the *Daily Universal Register,* by Mr. John Walter, the namesake and grandfather of the present principal proprietor, at Printing House Square.

He was an ingenious man, a master of the *technique* of printing, trying many doubtful experiments, and patenting various manifest improvements connected with his craft. On the first day of the year 1788, the paper appeared as *The ...*—the older and cumbrous title having proved as injurious to it as did Tristram to Mr. Shandy's son. To be "fashionable, humorous, and witty" entered into the design of Mr. Walter's organ in those early years, and it contained lively paragraphs such as now appear in the "society" papers. No leading articles were published then; and the number of advertisements in the first issue of *The Times* was only 57. Mr. Walter made the paper prosperous, and then transferred it in 1803 to his son, also a man of business knowledge and capacity. In 1810 *The Times* was certainly not open to that charge of trimming which has been advanced against it of late, with something of exaggeration; for its course was just then so unpleasant to the ruling politicians that the Government advertisements were withdrawn from its columns; and so petty became the persecution, that the editor's packages from abroad were stopped by Government at the outposts, while those for the Ministerial journals were allowed to pass. After successive enlargements, both in size and in circulation, *The Times* became difficult to produce in sufficient numbers by the hand printing-presses, and Mr. Walter, after expending much money and attention on attempts to meet the difficulty, at last produced, in 1814, a copy of the paper printed by steam and machinery—to the intense disgust of the pressmen in Printing House Square. *The Times* is now said to be produced, on the Walter printing-press, at the rate of more than 20,000 copies an hour, by a system over which something like £50,000 has been spent in bringing it to its present perfection. *The Times* has often acted with great public spirit, as when it did much to cure the first fever of railway speculation—at the loss of many thousands of pounds to its own coffers, through the retaliative withdrawal of these speculative advertisements from its columns. Thus has it earned its title of the Monarch of the Press. Its contributors (who are more handsomely paid than those of any other daily paper) include many eminent men in various walks of life; and its editor enjoys a prestige of his own among journalists and in general society. Of Mr. Delane, the late brilliant editor, we have spoken in earlier pages. His cessation of labour was followed by another severe loss to *The Times*—the retirement of its sub-editor, Mr. Stebbing. The present occupant of the editorial throne is Mr. Thomas Chenery, formerly known to fame only as a distinguished Oriental scholar.

Time (1, York Street, Covent Garden; Monthly, 1s.), a magazine of general literature, brightly edited by Mr. Edmund Yates.

Times Weekly Edition (2d.) has been published since 1877, containing prominent contents of one week's daily issues.

Tinsley's Magazine (8, Catherine Street, Strand; Monthly, 1s.) contains essays and reviews, but is chiefly known for its fiction—largely contributed of late by Mr. Richard Dowling, the young novelist whose "Mystery of Killard" and "Weird Sisters" have scored a signal success.

Truth (79, Queen Street, E.C.; Weekly, 6d.), started in 1877 by Mr. Labouchere. It has much in common with the *World*, devoting a large space to the political, personal, and cynical paragraphs of which everybody more or less protests that he disapproves, while everybody reads them. *Truth* is less literary than the *World*, caring less for classical finish or technical excellence than for spiciness and dash. The paper largely reflects the personality of the editor, who has an efficient lieutenant in Mr. Horace Voules.

Unitarian Publications:—1. *Christian Life* (123, Fleet Street; Weekly, 2d.) 2. *Inquirer* (37, Norfolk Street, Strand; Weekly, 5d.)

University Magazine (13, Great Marlborough Street; Monthly, 2s. 6d.), critical essays and reviews. Formerly the *Dublin University Magazine*.

Vanity Fair (12, Tavistock Street, W.C.; Weekly, 1s.), the first and

CORRECTED FOR PRESS.

Madras, to which Clive had been appointed, was, at this time, perhaps, the first in importance of the Company's settlements.

In the preceding century, Fort Saint George had arisen on a spot barren beaten by a raging surf, and in the neighbourhood a town, inhabited by many thousands of natives, had sprung up, as they spring up in the *East*, with the rapidity of the Prophet's gourd. There were already in the suburbs many white villas, each surrounded by its garden, whither the agents of the company retired, after the labours of the desk, to enjoy the cool breeze which springs up at sunset from the Bay of Bengal. The habits of these mercantile grandees appear to have been more profuse, luxurious, and ostentatious than those of the high judicial and political functionaries who have succeeded them. *Lord Clive,* by LORD MACAULAY.

HOW TO CORRECT PROOFS.

" MADRAS, to which CLIVE had been appointed, was, at this time, perhaps, the first in importance of the Company's settlements. In the preceding century, Fort *St. George* had arisen on a barren spot beaten by a raging surf; and in the neighbourhood a town, inhabited by many thousands of natives, had sprung up, as towns spring up in the East, with the rapidity of the prophet's gourd.

" There were already in the suburbs many white villas (each surrounded by its garden), whither the agents of the Company retired, after the labours of the desk and the warehouse, to enjoy the cool breeze which springs up at sunset from the Bay of Bengal. The habits of these mercantile grandees appear to have been more profuse, luxurious, and ostentatious than those of the high judicial and political functionaries who have succeeded them." — *Lord Clive, by* LORD MACAULAY.

HOW TO CORRECT PROOFS.

EXPLANATION.

1. Marks for turned commas, to designate extracts.

2. To change a word from small letters to capitals, mark three lines under it, and write *caps.* in the margin opposite.

3. Where there is a wrong letter, draw the pen through that letter, and mark the right one in the margin opposite, with a down line following it.

4. When a paragraph commences where it is not intended, connect the matter by a line, and write in the margin opposite, *no break* or *run on*.

5. Where a word has to be changed to italic, make a line under the word, and write *italic* in the margin.

6. Words to be transposed.

7. A semi-colon omitted.

8. Omission of a word is noticed by a caret, $\wedge$ and marking in the margin.

9. To draw the letters of a word close together which stand apart.

10. The marks for a paragraph, when its commencement has been omitted.

11. Substitution of a capital for a small letter.

12. The substitution of a full point for a comma or other point.

13. Superfluous letters or words should be noticed by a line drawn through them, and this mark written in the margin (*dele*, take out).

14. The marks for closing an extract.

15. To change a word from small letters to small capitals, make two lines under the word, and write *sm. caps.* in the margin.

16. A letter turned upside down.

17. The mark for a space where it has been omitted between two words.

18. A comma omitted.

19. When a letter of a different size to that used, or of a different face, appears in a word, draw a line either through it or under it, and write opposite *w.f.* (wrong fount).

20. When one or more words have been struck out, and it is subsequently decided that they shall remain, make dots under them and write *stet* (stand) in the margin.

21. The substitution of one word for another.

22. Where a word has to be changed from Italic to Roman, make a line under it and write *roman* on the margin opposite.

23. The substitution of a small for a capital letter.

24. Marks when lines and words do not appear straight.

25. The marks for parentheses.

26. A battered, broken, or misshapen letter may also be noticed by a line drawn under or through it, and a + written in the margin.

27. Where a space stands up and appears, draw a line through it, and make a strong perpendicular mark in the margin.

28. A letter omitted.

29. The transposition of letters in a word.

30. The dash omitted. The hyphen omitted is marked by a shorter line with only one vertical mark.

31. The manner of marking an omission, or an insertion, when it is too long to be written in the side margin. When this occurs, it may be written either at the top or bottom of the page.

Care should always be taken that the *errata* are written in the order in which they occur.

INDEX.